"Erica Reid has written a wise and wonderful cookbook with recipes that promote heart health and brain health. We are what we eat and this book makes healthy eating for the whole family accessible and tasty!"

—*Gayatri Devi, MD, MS, FAAN,*
author of **A Calm Brain**

Shut Up and Cook!

ERICA REID

Shut Up and Cook!

MODERN, HEALTHY RECIPES THAT ANYONE CAN MAKE AND EVERYONE WILL LOVE

BenBella

BenBella Books, Inc.
Dallas, TX

BenBella

BenBella Books, Inc.
10440 N. Central Expressway, Suite 800
Dallas, TX 75231
www.benbellabooks.com
Send feedback to feedback@benbellabooks.com

Printed in the United States of America
10 9 8 7 6 5 4 3 2 1

Library of Congress Cataloging-in-Publication Data is available upon request.
978-1-942952-50-3 (trade paperback)
978-1-942952-51-0 (e-book)

All photos taken by Nicole Garner Photography
All photos styled by Hayley Christopher unless otherwise noted.
Photos on xiii, 1, 7, 115, 121, 125, 127, 147, 161, 169, 178, and 192 styled by Nicole Garner Photography
Editing by Scott Calamar and Leah Wilson
Copyediting by Elizabeth Degenhard
Proofreading by Kimberly Broderick and Jenny Bridges

Indexing by WordCo Indexing Services
Text design and composition by Kit Sweeney
Cover design by Sarah Dombrowsky
Distributed by Perseus Distribution
www.perseusdistribution.com

To place orders through Perseus Distribution:
Tel: (800) 343-4499
Fax: (800) 351-5073
E-mail: orderentry@perseusbooks.com

Special discounts for bulk sales (minimum of 25 copies) are available.
Please contact Aida Herrera at aida@benbellabooks.com.

Dedicated to health, to those with food
challenges, to those who lost their lives
innocently to food allergies, and of course,
to you, for picking up this cookbook!

"YOU MUST DO
THE THINGS
YOU THINK YOU
CANNOT DO."

—*Eleanor Roosevelt*

Contents

Dear Friend and Cook xiii

Introduction: Stop Talking. Start Cooking 1

Helpful and Healthful Cooking Tips

The Tools 8

The Food and Ingredients 11

Foods You Won't Find 13

Basic Principles of Buying and
Preparing Your Food 16

RECIPES

Breakfast

Blueberry or Chocolate Chip Spelt Muffins . . 22

Antioxidant Fruit Salad 24

Carrot Raisin Muffins 25

Summer Watermelon Fruit Bowl 26

Dairy-Free Challah Vanilla French Toast 29

Granola Brittle 31

Saturday Morning Spelt and Oat Pancakes . . 32

Huevos Rancheros (Egg or Extra-Firm Tofu)
with Black Beans 34

Cozy Millet and Brown Rice Porridge 36

Vegetarian

Snack-Time Tofu Dip with Crudités 38

Home-Run Gazpacho 39

Cauliflower Rice Salad with
Green Beans and Chickpeas 40

Rice-Free Cauliflower Sushi Rolls 42

Orange and Fennel Salad 45

Garden Arugula Green Bean Salad 46

New York Bowl 47

The Hollywood Bowl 48

Backyard Pickled Vegetables 51

Load 'em Up Vegetable Stir-Fry 52

Harvest Acorn Squash with Cinnamon
Maple Syrup 54

Yum-Yum Black Beans 55

Mother Earth Collard Green Wraps 57

Zucchini and Carrot Pasta 58

Soul-Warming Black-Eyed Peas 61

Black Bean Mango Salad with a Kick 62

Coconut Rice 64

Kelp Noodle Stir-Fry 65

Avocado Carrot Salad 67

Fry-Free Veggie Spring Rolls 68

Black Bean Burgers 70

Canada Cauliflower 73

Tofu Veggie Burritos 74

Poultry

City Jerk Chicken 76

Turkey Tacos 77

Bun-less Turkey Burgers 79

Mama's Turkey Meatballs 81

Game-Day Buffalo Chicken Wings 82

Chicken in the Garden, LA's Favorite 85

Turkey Bacon–Wrapped Asparagus 86

Family Turkey Meatloaf 88

Mom's Bliss Pelau Chicken, My Way 91

Lamb and Other Meats

Mom's Staple Kielbasa with Sauerkraut . . . 95

Rosemary Lamb Chops 96

Savory Lamb Burgers 98

Fish

Ginger Salmon 100

Miso Cod en Papillote 103

Salmon "Sushi" Rolls 104
Gluten-Free Salmon Pea Pasta 105

Dressings and Sauces

Avocado Dressing 108
Lemon Dressing 110
Herbed Salad Dressing 111
Teriyaki Sauce 112
Maple Cider Vinaigrette 113
Plum Sauce 114

Soups

Broth 116
Black Bean Soup 117
Green Soup 119
Shredded "Soup-Kitchen" Chicken Soup . 120
Cauliflower Soup 122
Soothing Butternut Soup 123

Pizza

With Love, Arianna and Addison's Pizza . 126
Three-Cheese Veggie Pizza 128
Pesto Avocado Pizza 129

Snacks

Nana's Rolls, My Way 132
Toasted Nori and Sea Salt Popcorn 134
Double-Dip Black Bean Dip 135
Garlic Boost Spread 136
Gypsy Girl Guacamole 137
Sweet Potato Fries with Rosemary 139
Parsnip Fries 140
Honeymoon Salsa 141
Modern Focaccia Bread 143

Chips: Zucchini, Mushroom,
Brussels Sprouts, and Beet 144
French-Style Radishes with Nondairy Butter 146

Desserts

Chocolate Chip Cookies with Crispy Kale . 149
Grandma's Nondairy Sweet Potato Pie . . . 150
Guilt-Free Doughnuts 152
Watermelon Granita 153
Nondairy Strawberry Ice Cream 154
Pineapple Lemon Granita 156
Childhood Bundt Cake 157
Scrumptious Sweet Apple Pie 159
Soy Butter Rice Krispies® Cups 160
Cinnamon Saturday Apple Crisp 163
Vegan Cheesecake 164
Decadent Chocolate Truffles 166
Balsamic Strawberries with Basil 167
Raspberry Strawberry Soup 168

Drinks

Green Juice 170
Raspberry Sorbet with Sparkling Water . . . 171
Cooling Watermelon Juice 172
Tropical Fruit Smoothie 173
Avocado Kale Smoothie 174

Acknowledgments 178
Index 183
About the Author 191

Dear Friend and Cook,

Like many of you, I love to help people. I love teaching. I love to share, especially a great way of eating, or a divine recipe, or a health tip that can boost awareness. This is why I want to share this cookbook with you, your family, and your friends—to help make a wonderful difference in your health and life. For this reason, I'm sharing not only my easy and delicious recipes with you, but also my journey, my fears, and my mistakes. My hope is that these recipes and stories benefit you and your loved ones by boosting your confidence, your creativity, and your knowledge—so this book becomes part of your journey.

My mission, plain and simple, is to show you how you can still get your grub on in a healthier way, without depriving yourself. It's also to help you from feeling lost in your own kitchen. I admit, I've been lost plenty of times. I knew how to keep my home clean, how to keep my children's lives organized, and how to whip together a last-minute glam outfit to wear to a star-studded event. But I felt helpless in the kitchen.

I didn't know how to make my kitchen work for me, my family, and our visiting friends. I did not know how to use it other than as a social gathering room—a place to pour glasses of water or play a card game on the table.

And, honestly, I believed it required more effort and way more time to cook something scrumptious and healthy than it did to order takeout. With two kids and a busy life, the last thing I wanted to do was spend all my time cooking.

But I was wrong. I was letting my fear override my instinct. I was avoiding cooking—avoiding nourishing the people I love—because I was scared of making mistakes. And, even beyond the fear, I didn't have a clue as to where or how to start.

In my journey, I learned I always had a cook inside of me—just like there's a cook inside of you. I hid mine, covering it up and keeping it from blossoming—just like you might be hiding yours. But it's time to stop avoiding your kitchen, like I did, and make healthier choices; it's time to actually start using your pots and pans.

To become the cook I am today, I just needed a push to trust my instincts, just like we all need a good push from time to time. Consider this my gift to you—a push into your cooking journey, and into your kitchen. Use these recipes as a foundation for your learning, for experimentation, and for the discoveries you'll make along the way. Use my stories to know that none of us are perfect, but all of us want to be our best, and we're only going to get there when we trust our instincts.

You can do this. You're going to be great. Shut up and cook!

With much love and confidence,

Introduction: Stop Talking. Start Cooking.

What does it mean to *Shut Up and Cook*? It means shut up and cook. Shut up with the excuses, shut up with the fears. Get out of your head and into your kitchen!

You want to look and feel your best, but you don't have the time, motivation, or tools to live healthier? This book is for you. Your gut instinct has been telling you that you need to pay more attention to the food you're putting into your body, but you find it hard, in today's world, to argue with convenience? This book is for you.

This book is for young and old, married with kids, or enjoying the single life. It's for anyone who wants to make a change or take control. It's for people living on the Paleo diet. It's for vegetarians and vegans. It's for meat eaters. It's for snackers and diet slackers. It's for those of you who already know your way around a cutting board and those of you who don't even know where to start. No matter what you eat, or what your level of skill, this book is for you.

This book is not about what *not* to eat; it's about *how* to make the food you cook healthier. It's about showing you that cooking, especially healthier cooking, can be easy, quick, and delicious. (Most of the recipes here take less than 45 minutes to make!) And, most importantly, this book is about turning off the voice of fear, confusion, and anxiety in your head—the one that comes from being so overloaded with information about which foods are and are not healthy that you give up before you even begin.

This book is for you, because it will become your cookbook. Of course, to begin with, this book is filled with recipes I've created throughout the years for myself and my family. But the purpose of this book isn't to guide you into my way of eating. The purpose is to guide you into *your* way of eating, through *my* way of cooking—a process of experimentation that allows you to eat what you love and be healthier at the same time.

You want easy recipes that will help you feed yourself, your family, and your friends—every day, and while entertaining—in a healthy way. They're in here. I'll help you face your initial fears. I'll provide simple-to-make recipes. I'll provide healthier options, which you can take or leave. But, at the end of the day, you need to make these recipes yours. You need to make them for yourself and your family and friends, and tweak them for *your* needs. My goal for you is to make this book yours—for you to own your food, your kitchen, and your health.

This book is your book. So dive in, shut up, and cook.

WHY ME? HOW'D I END UP WRITING A COOKBOOK?

At some point we all get a wake-up call—a voice that whispers to us that we need change, or booms from our scale when fifteen new pounds of weight seem to appear without reason. Some of us get wake-up calls when we develop food sensitivities. Some of us, maybe a little later in life, get that wake-up call when a doctor warns us about health problems: high blood pressure, high blood sugar, or cholesterol.

My wake-up call was my kids. They seemed to always be sick—skin rashes, tummy troubles, gut irritability, sinus issues, upper respiratory challenges, colds in 80-degree weather, or other strange ailments. At first, it didn't occur to me that our health might have anything to do with what we were eating. I made no connection. Food was food and health was health. They were totally separate, I thought. But boy was I so wrong. That's when I asked myself, *How is the food we eat affecting my family?*

Here I am having fun in the kitchen. Be daring. Be happy. Be healthier.

And, what can I do about it?

The simple solution was to be aware of how my kids responded to consuming certain foods, and when I did indeed notice something (which I most often did), I removed that food or ingredient from their diet.

As I started to do this more and more with them and noticed a huge positive difference in their health, I thought, *Well, I have issues too.* These were things that I usually never paid much attention to: acne, stomach bloat (which frequently led to the need to unbutton my skirt or pants while dining out!), sleepiness after eating certain foods, and often a sore throat. Slowly, I began removing foods from my own diet that were causing me to feel more negative than positive. If something made me feel bloated, or tired, or itchy, it was gone.

I was eliminating foods from both my kids' and my diet like a mad woman. However, I also quickly noticed the joy of eating was being eliminated from our lives as well.

During this experience, I learned about food sensitivities. And I realized that I was making us all feel yucky by depending on outside food that I was not cooking, or frozen packaged items full of ingredients that, though I could read them on the label, I didn't really understand.

That little voice—the same one that told me I needed to cut certain foods out of my family's diet—returned one day as my son was paging through a themed cookbook for one of his favorite movies. I noticed the look on his face was pure excitement. Each page held beautiful photographs of scrumptious-looking treats that would leave even the healthiest eaters drooling for a bite. And there was my son asking me to make the item on each new page he turned. "Mommy, can you make me this? Mommy, can you make me that?"

While I did not know *how* to make any of those recipes, I said, "Of course." I was not going to deprive my children. Just because the recipes on those pages were off-limits due to his food sensitivities and food allergies shouldn't have to mean he should be left out of the fun. That little voice—the same one that told me to cut out the junk—

gave me another wake-up call. It said, *You can figure out a way to make those recipes for him.*

I already had a nice kitchen. I never used it, though. I didn't understand it. But that voice told me to figure it out. The voice said, *There's the kitchen. There are tools in the kitchen. Just try, Erica.*

Honestly, before I got in the kitchen, I had no idea glass measuring cups were to measure liquids and the round silver measuring devices with handles were for dry ingredients like flour. I didn't know the language of cooking, either. What's a "scant"? What's a "dollop"? I didn't know; I'd never heard of them. I had to look them up. And, if you would have asked me years ago what the odds were of me, Erica Reid, writing a cookbook, my answer would have been zero.

Recipe attempt after recipe attempt ensued. I tried. I often failed. I tried again. And, over time, I began finding solutions, variations, and tricks. I found ways to make healthier versions of the foods we actually wanted to eat—including many of the treats in my son's movie cookbook. And, even more importantly, I came to a realization about the importance of the kitchen to my family's health. I refer to my refrigerator as the medicine cabinet, and the kitchen as my home pharmacy. It's where we find fuel, positive or negative. The foods you eat can energize you or make you feel sleepy and less focused. They can harm or they can heal. We have a choice about our health, because we have a choice about what we eat.

Why me? Why my cookbook? Because I was you. I did the research. I scoured the internet for information. I learned as much as I could.

I wish someone would have written this exact same book for me back then. I wish someone would have asked me the same question I'm going to ask you: Is there a way to make the foods you love and crave but make them healthier?

HOW SHOULD YOU READ AND USE THIS BOOK?

This book is intended to be in the kitchen with you; it's not a decorated coffee table book. It's intended to get messy. I mean it when I say, "Shut up and cook." I don't want to get overcomplicated. I don't want you to feel anxious like I did about getting into the kitchen. In fact, in this book, I've included short stories about how and why my recipes were created. You don't have to read the stories. But if you choose to read them, you'll see a common theme—one of me finding something I love, my family loves, or my friends love, going into the kitchen to figure out how I can make what they love without all the guilt. You'll

Shut Up and Flip

If you're looking for something you can take On the Go, just look for this Easy Flip icon:

Just because you're leaving your house and traveling by subway, bus, train, car, plane, or roller skate doesn't mean you can't have nourishing food. Prepare it at home to take with you on the go! This icon will help you find foods that you can take with you to work or on a trip. These recipes are also great for bringing with you to a baby shower or a potluck, taking to someone who is feeling under the weather, or giving someone a special treat made with lots of love and with great health in mind.

also notice that many of the recipes I included are those that I grew up with, which I made healthier. But those are my stories. I want you to create your own stories.

You might also wonder why I choose not to use some ingredients, cook things in certain ways, use certain tools over others, or add specific ingredients. The sections that follow will cover most of the reasons I cook the way I cook, but throughout this book, I've also included motivational tips which I call **SHUT UP AND LISTEN** segments. Again, you don't have to read the tips. You can just cook. I don't want to bog you down with words, but I also don't want to leave you with unanswered questions.

I had tons of questions myself when I started cooking. There was so much I didn't know and did not understand. For instance, the math part of having to measure some items was so freakin' *hard* for me to figure out at times. Of course, I've done a lot of testing and experimenting over the years. And, I've come to the realization that we

don't need to know every detail and scientific fact about food—we just need simple explanations. With this in mind, I've included **Did You Know?** segments in this book—short, straightforward explanations and insights I've learned during my cooking and health journey.

My ultimate goal is to make you comfortable with trying new things and making this book your book. So I include options with certain recipes. But I'm not the "option police." If you have an idea that you want to try—an ingredient you think would improve a recipe for you and your family—I urge you to try it. Mix it up. Make it yours. Use the special COOK'S NOTES section—a blank area that you can and should write in—with each recipe to create your own versions of my recipes. You could even include why you choose to use certain ingredients over others. Again, the goal is to make this, and your food, yours.

Enough talking. Enough thinking. Enough is enough. It's time to get in the kitchen. It's time to take control. It's time to *Shut Up and Cook.*

Helpful and Healthful Cooking Tips

There's more to cooking than just turning on a stovetop or pressing the buttons of a food processor. But don't worry if your kitchen and your cooking tools feel foreign to you (for instance, if you have no clue what that long knife is supposed to cut, or what that funny thing that looks like a spring is supposed to do). Just let your instincts guide you. You'll figure it out. At this stage of the game, when it comes to tools, the only thing that matters is how those implements might affect the health quality of your food. However, as you cook, you'll learn what feels more right for specific tasks—stir with a fork or use a whisk, for instance. Grab things and try them out. While the tools you use aren't really important, they may make cooking easier.

On the next pages are some general things I've learned about tools in my journey through the kitchen. You may not need to read this now. But hold on to it, dog-ear it, and come back to it if necessary.

Did You Know?

Some experts say the intestinal issue known as "leaky gut" has a direct connection to what you are eating.

Did You Know?

Some foods can cause eczema, a severe skin irritation.

THE TOOLS

POTS AND PANS: I try to cook the majority of my family's food in a cast-iron skillet. My mother once told me you get the nutrient "iron" from cooking in iron. I am not sure how true that is or isn't, but I like the idea of it, so I do it. (I once had low iron levels, but no longer do, and I believe there is a connection.) I recall that my ninety-three-year-young grandmother, Nana, always made her okra and her homemade cornbread in her cast-iron skillet. Of course, cast-iron skillets have been around for many years and used over and over again, from generation to generation. I prefer to cook with pans that are not chemically treated; I don't use nonstick pans. I strongly believe that when our pots and pans are heated, they release whatever chemical is used to make that vessel, and those chemicals may seep into the food. Of course, this reaction is not visible, so it's not like you're going to see that chemical being cooked and mixed into your food. I'm not going to suggest that you avoid nonstick or chemically treated pans, but I am going to mention it to you because I want to share that awareness. The same may be true about certain metals with low melting points, such as aluminum.

CUTTING BOARDS: I prefer to use bamboo wood cutting boards. Again, there are no chemicals being sliced and diced into my foods as I prepare them, like with the plastic boards that now say they are no longer made with any bisphenol A (BPA). BPA is an "organic synthetic" compound long used in plastics; its presence in foods has been possibly linked to high blood pressure and other health issues. Perhaps it's harmless, but if they're touting plastic without it, someone must have doubts about it. And it probably means those plastic boards that aren't labeled may include this compound. All in all, I just prefer natural when it comes to food preparation.

WOODEN SPOONS: I learned many years ago when eating a macrobiotic diet that food, too, has energy and what comes in contact with our food is important. I try not to use spatulas and cooking utensils that have rubber ends, which can melt when they heat up. Imagine what that melted chemical is seeping into. It is definitely not going straight into the air, so … where? Yep, your *food*.

The food you buy is the food you eat. Shop wisely and make your life and your diet as colorful and fresh as possible!

THE FOOD AND INGREDIENTS

When it comes to flavor and nutrition, I've put years of trial and error into this book. Decades of tasting and testing healthy foods are the foundation of these recipes. But you'll also find healthy doses of reality mixed in. Not everything is 100 percent free of preservatives. Today's world calls for us to be practical and realistic, always keeping health in mind.

Some of the ingredients in this book will be familiar, and some may be new to you. Do not be afraid! Give them a chance. You may surprise yourself. The point is to eat the way that works best for you, and don't shy away from new ingredients that could become staples of your diet. Many of the recipes in this book would not have come to fruition if I did not try out some new ingredients.

Here are just a few of the ingredients included in this book known for their health benefits, which you might not be familiar with:

ARAME: A type of sea oak that is a species of kelp frequently used in Japanese dishes; it's loaded with minerals.

KOMBU: An edible form of kelp widely eaten in East Asia.

UMEBOSHI PASTE: A pickled plum puree that can be found at Whole Foods and most Asian grocery stores.

UMEBOSHI VINEGAR: A by-product of a red Japanese plum (closely related to apricots but pickled—pucker up!) used in many Japanese dishes. It is also known as ume plum vinegar.

DRY LOTUS ROOT: A root vegetable rich in nutrients, known in Japan as renkon. It offers a lot of photo-nutrients, minerals, and vitamin C.

APPLE CIDER VINEGAR: A type of vinegar made from apple cider; it has many health benefits.

NONDAIRY BUTTER: A dairy-free and, if you choose, soy-free vegan substitution for butter (a gluten-free option is also available).

SOY "PEANUT" BUTTER: A butter spread made from roasted soy beans rather than peanuts.

KOSHER SALT: Pure salt is always technically kosher because it is a mineral. However, a kosher label means the salt has been inspected for its purity.

SEA SALT: A salt derived from the process of evaporating sea water.

SEA VEG: A seaweed-based ingredient used for imparting flavor and nutrition. I personally use the brand Sea Seasonings® by Maine Coast (which is Sea Salt, Kelp, and Dulse). It is also a great source of iodine.

NONDAIRY CHEESE BY FOLLOW YOUR HEART®: A vegan substitute for traditional dairy cheeses.

EGG REPLACER: A vegan substitute for eggs.

TOFU: A bean curd made from coagulated soy milk; it is dairy free.

TEMPEH: A soy product, originating from Indonesia, made by a natural fermentation process that binds soybeans into a solid form (almost like a cake or burger patty).

TURMERIC: A spice derived from the ginger family; it has a peppery bitterness and is widely used for its health benefits and distinctive flavor.

FOODS YOU WON'T FIND

I've just told you about some of the ingredients you will find in these recipes. But I also avoid some very common foods, and I think it's important for me to tell you why I personally don't ever—or rarely ever—use them in my recipes. Again, that doesn't mean you can't. Please realize that I created these recipes for me and my family, and you should be inspired to create your own for your family.

TABLE SALT: It's no secret that too much salt can be unhealthy for us. Excessive salt has been linked to high blood pressure and heart disease. However, some health professionals suggest that we do need some salt, as it is an important nutrient (iodine) and helps with thyroid wellness. For me, I just like how my recipes taste without much salt, so I rarely use common table salt. When I do cook or wash fruits and vegetables, I'll use sea salt because salt pulls excess dirt or pesticides from vegetables when used with cold water. And, for most recipes that need it, I'll flavor with FarmaSea Sea Veg, which contains natural sea salt.

EGGS: Many experts suggest that egg allergies are one of the most common food allergies and can cause skin conditions, respiratory problems, and severe stomach pain in many people. I typically do not use eggs in my recipes because my son was once allergic to eggs. So, naturally, I vowed to make as many of my recipes as possible egg free. You don't have to be allergic or vegan to avoid eggs; many people are simply not fans of them. But, if you're fine with eggs, use them. In recipes without eggs where eggs are an option, I'll tell you. For instance,

Did You Know?

When dining out, if you're concerned that your family has allergies to nuts, ask a restaurant if they cook in nut-based oils.

my recipe for Huevos Rancheros on page 34 shows you two ways to make it: with and without egg.

MEAT: Meat has received its fair share of health criticism over the past few decades, with many professionals linking it to heart disease and high blood pressure, or expressing concern about the excessive hormone levels added to our livestock. Nevertheless, I personally don't include much red meat in my recipes because it's my choice not to eat beef or pork or to feed it to my family. It's been a lifestyle for me for so long (I stopped eating meat in college) that, well, I don't have any recipes that use beef or pork. Of course, it's your personal decision to eat or avoid meats. I'm sure beef or pork could be added to a few recipes in this book.

NUTS: I personally do not use nuts in my recipes as I am allergic to tree nuts (I can eat peanuts, though I don't consume them because of my children's nut allergies), and I feel for the millions and millions of people in the world with this severe life-threatening allergy. If it were up to me, any restaurant or food place that served nuts to the public would have to clearly list it on their menus so patrons would be informed. Airlines would not be able to serve such danger at 37,000 feet. Nuts are deadly to millions of people. DEADLY. So none of the recipes in this book include them. Of course, if you want to add nuts to anything in here, please feel free to do so at your own risk! *If you're serving any type of nut (peanut, tree nut, something cooked with nut oils) to loved ones or during a social gathering at your home, be sure to ask if anyone is allergic to nuts. Also make this ingredient known before putting any nut-based food on a plate and serving it.*

GLUTEN: Millions of people are gluten sensitive and don't even realize it. Gluten intolerance can cause consistent abdominal pain and bloating, breathing problems, and even anxiety in some cases. I try to eat gluten free, at least at home, because at one point I overate foods with glutens and became severely sensitive to it. If I dine out, I still try not to overload on foods that contain gluten. Again, it's my choice to avoid it, and some of my recipes reflect that. If you're OK with gluten, feel free to exercise your own options. *If you have celiac challenges or if you are on a strict gluten-free diet, always consult with your health practitioner. I am only sharing my personal experience— do seek your own personal professional assistance.*

DAIRY: You'll notice that most of the recipes in this book are dairy free as well, and that's because my son and I are sensitive to dairy. In fact, many people are sensitive to dairy but don't realize some of the side effects like increased mucus production, upset stomach, skin irritations, and gas. Obviously, if dairy doesn't bother you, you can choose to put it back into the recipes where I skip it.

NIGHTSHADE VEGETABLES: Someone once explained to me that nightshade vegetables grow at night or in the shade. That freaked me out—I've always known the sun to nourish our growing fruits and vegetables. I'll use nightshade vegetables in a few recipes, but because some experts suggest these foods may cause inflammation, arthritis, and even depression in some people, I try not to use them. Some of the common nightshade vegetables are tomatoes, eggplants, peppers, and white potatoes.

CORN: In my opinion, corn is too frequently used to feed animals and livestock, and it's common in so many daily food items, like cereal, that I try to minimize it in my cooking. Many people have reactions to corn including sneezing, stuffy head, hives, stomach irritation, and eczema. Also, corn can be hard for the intestines to process. I don't like the idea of putting anything in my body that is difficult to digest.

Did You Know?

Gluten is the "glue" that helps certain foods hold their form. It sticks together and it sticks to you, as well. It is a type of protein that many individuals are sensitive to, though they may not know it. Gluten is found in breads, cereals, crackers, condiments, pastas, baked desserts such as cakes, cookies and donuts, and many packaged foods (unless specified "gluten free").

BASIC PRINCIPLES OF BUYING AND PREPARING YOUR FOOD

LEARN HOW TO GROCERY SHOP: In America, most of our grocery stores are designed so that the fruit and the vegetables (which are known as the produce) are on the outside aisles of the grocery store. The inside aisles, which I like to refer to as the "maze" aisles (because we are constantly walking around and around trying to find items), stock all the packaged food. Try to avoid spending too much time in the maze aisles because many of those foods are the processed ones—less healthy than the produce. Aim to fill your cart with live, fresh, colorful foods. Just like your refrigerator, your shopping cart is a container—it reveals your health future. If you do buy some packaged foods, try adding fresh ingredients to them to provide some nutrients, as advised in some of the recipes.

FARM TO TABLE: Food from farm to table is not new (humans have been eating this way for thousands of years) but for some reason we are making this a recent innovation. This is how my ninety-three-year-young Nana ate, and this is how I believe we are supposed to eat. I prefer a plant-based diet. I have personally witnessed firsthand the health benefits of eating fresh. Yes, I know it is hard, and it may be impossible to have a farm or a garden in your backyard. For those who can't, you can visit community farmers' markets. We *all* deserve to have access to clean, fresh, non-toxic food. We are all entitled to good health.

AVOID THE MIX: I try not to mix vegetables and fruits together. I know that some cultures and countries—as well as certain diets and eating traditions—do not believe in mixing, either. Personally, I have found that mixing can sometimes cause me to feel a bit bloated or irritable, or to have an uncomfortable belly. So I am cautious of what fruits and vegetables I am combining, and I pay close attention to how I feel after I eat the mix. You might feel fine. My system is sensitive. I simply want to make you aware.

FOOD OVER PILLS: I personally believe that our food is our only source of true nourishment. Take a moment to consider the side effects of pills produced by pharmaceutical companies—or even your vitamin pills. Are they toxic? Can they be harmful to your organs in the long run? I try to go for what God made that comes from Mother Earth, not from any factory. But, of course, do what suits you best.

RECIPES

Breakfast

Blueberry or Chocolate Chip Spelt Muffins

YIELD: 12 MUFFINS (6 CHOCOLATE AND 6 BLUEBERRY) These are some of my children's favorite home-baked items—and I'm sure they will soon become favorites of you and your loved ones as well. Spelt flour is easier to digest than white flour. Due to some of my food sensitivities, spelt has allowed me to eat these tasty treats when I once had to limit many baked items. I played around and made these a few different ways—for different tastes. You can experiment with the recipe to make your favorite flavors of muffin!

1 teaspoon coconut oil or olive oil, for pan

3 ripe bananas, peeled

½ teaspoon baking soda

⅓ cup rice milk

¼ cup maple syrup

2 tablespoons olive oil

2 teaspoons pure vanilla extract

1 teaspoon apple cider vinegar

2 cups spelt flour

2 teaspoons baking powder

1 teaspoon ground cinnamon

½ cup blueberries or vegan chocolate chips

1. Preheat oven to 350 degrees F. Grease the cups of a muffin pan with coconut oil and set aside.

2. In a medium bowl, add the ripe bananas and smash, using a fork, until pureed; mix in the baking soda. Next, pour in the rice milk, maple syrup, olive oil, pure vanilla extract, and apple cider vinegar; give the entire mixture a good stir. Add the spelt flour, baking powder, and cinnamon, and mix just until the speckles of flour are no longer visible.

3. At this point you have a few options. You can divide the batter in two by adding half to a medium bowl. Fold in ¼ cup blueberries to one bowl and ¼ cup chocolate chips to the other. This will give you two types of muffins. Or, you can fold ½ cup blueberries or ½ cup chocolate chips into the entire big batch of batter.

4. Divide the batter among the muffin cups, filling them up about halfway. Transfer the muffins to the oven to bake for 20 to 25 minutes. Remove from the oven and allow to cool completely in the pan. Run a knife alongside the outside of each muffin—they should pop right out!

COOK'S NOTES

Blueberry
Spelt Muffins

INTUITIVE MOMENTS

I think this is the one recipe in this book that I struggled over and over again to perfect. But when I did get it exactly as I liked it, the result was absolutely amazing. In fact, it was so good, that for a while I didn't share it.

Everyone loves muffins. I remember seeing some muffins in a bakery window when my kids were younger, and thinking, "I bet they would love those." Then I remember thinking, "I'm going to find a way to make muffins for my children."

I went home that day on a mother's mission and started playing. The first batch was a bit of a joke but OK. The second got better, but not quite there. The third was pretty good. But they still weren't perfect. So I kept making them over and over, yet they weren't quite right yet. Then one of my kids wanted blueberry muffins. The other wanted chocolate chips. And I wanted to keep testing variations of the batter until I figured out how to split the recipes so each could have their favorite.

I was proud of what I'd come up with. I started to bake them and share them as a surprise with close friends. I started telling people about them. And so did other people. Friends of my kids would tell their parents about the muffins they ate during sleepovers at our home. Parents began contacting me, saying their kids who never ate breakfast would only eat my muffins. They started asking for the recipe. And I felt pretty protective of it. I've shared plenty of my muffins but never this recipe until now. Enjoy them!

Antioxidant Fruit Salad ✈

SERVES 4 Antioxidants are an immune booster like nothing else. Especially in a world that is becoming more and more toxic and polluted, I try to combat invaders with this unbelievably delicious and sweet fruit salad. It's great for breakfast but also makes a wonderful side dish for a light lunch.

2 pints raspberries

1 pint blueberries

Juice from 1 naval orange

Juice from ½ lime

8 mint leaves, minced, plus a few more for garnish

1. In a large bowl, toss together the raspberries, blueberries, orange juice, lime juice, and minced mint leaves.

2. Garnish with a few whole mint leaves.

Did You Know?

Antioxidants are known to fight against the daily radiation that we face in our environment.

COOK'S NOTES

Carrot Raisin Muffins ✈

YIELD: 12 MUFFINS Carrots in muffins? Don't run from the thought. The carrot adds not only a bit of natural color variation and a bit of nutrients to ease the guilt, but also a natural sweetness. For those of you who have ever tried carrot juice (or eaten carrot cake!), you know what I mean.

1. Preheat oven to 350 degrees F. Grease the cups of a muffin pan with the coconut oil or olive oil, and set aside.

2. In a large bowl, whisk together the spelt flour, baking powder, baking soda, cinnamon, shredded carrot, and raisins. Set aside.

3. In a medium bowl, mix together the applesauce, rice milk, maple syrup, olive oil, pure vanilla extract, and apple cider vinegar. In one batch, pour the wet ingredients into the dry and mix until speckles of flour are no longer visible.

4. Divide the batter among the muffin cups, filling them up about ¾ full. Transfer the muffins to the oven to bake for 20 to 25 minutes. Remove from the oven and allow to cool completely in the pan. Run a knife alongside the outside of the muffin—they should pop right out!

1 teaspoon coconut oil or olive oil, for pan

2 cups spelt flour

2 teaspoons baking powder

½ teaspoon baking soda

1 teaspoon ground cinnamon

1 cup shredded carrot (from about 1 carrot)

½ cup raisins

1 cup applesauce

¼ cup rice milk

¼ cup plus 2 tablespoons maple syrup

¼ cup olive oil

2 teaspoons pure vanilla extract

1 teaspoon apple cider vinegar

COOK'S NOTES

Summer Watermelon Fruit Bowl

SERVES 8 TO 12 This is one of my favorite recipes. I simply cannot get enough of it because it's so refreshing. This fruit bowl is loaded with many nutrients such as antioxidants. The natural sweetness from the fruit makes it a great dessert or even ideal to consume as a morning bite or early-day nibble.

1 (6-pound) seedless watermelon

1 cup (from ¼ pineapple) chopped pineapple

1 pint raspberries

1 pint blueberries

1 kiwi, peeled and sliced

1 plum, seed removed and sliced

Juice from 1 lime

Handful of mint leaves, for garnish

1. Start by cutting a thin slice from the bottom of the watermelon with a sharp knife so it can sit flat, making sure not to cut a hole in the bottom. Cut off the top ¼ from the watermelon. Using a melon baller, scoop balls of watermelon. Reserve the watermelon for serving.

2. In a bowl, toss together the watermelon balls, pineapple, raspberries, blueberries, kiwi, plum, and lime juice. Add as much of this fruit salad to the watermelon boat as will fit (you'll have some extra) and top with a few mint leaves as garnish. Place the extra fruit salad in the refrigerator and serve the watermelon boat immediately. Refill as needed.

COOK'S NOTES

Shut Up and Listen

Cook a meal that is going to do your body well. That's such a simple solution to eating healthier. After all, are you eating to feel yucky afterward? No! You're eating to feel fabulous, nourished, and energized!

INTUITIVE MOMENTS

Fruit salad was a treat in my home when I was growing up, especially when we were entertaining guests. My mom worked full time and her shifts were always changing. Sometimes she worked in the morning and sometimes at night. Either way, no matter what her work schedule, she always found the time to create the most beautiful and nutritious fruit bowls—vibrant with color and rich with vitamins and flavor. Mom always had a way of putting her creative touch into her fruit bowls, and those brilliant creations are the inspiration behind this recipe.

Did You Know?

When you choose a dairy-free option, you can avoid a possible sore throat reaction and help reduce inflammation in the body.

Dairy-Free Challah Vanilla French Toast

SERVES 2 TO 4 Milk causes problems for many people. It certainly does for me and some of my family members. I once thought I had to add milk to stretch and expand the batter to accommodate making more. But, with a little experimentation, I found this requires no milk at all. The bread you choose in this recipe is also key. I love a good challah bread, because the texture is soft and it absorbs nicely, but get the bread you like and prefer.

1. Heat the olive oil in a medium sauté pan set over medium heat.

2. Slice the challah bread into 1-inch-thick pieces.

3. In a medium bowl, crack in the eggs and whisk in the vanilla bean, pure vanilla extract, and ground cinnamon. Dip the slices of challah bread into the batter and transfer to the warm sauté pan. Cook on both sides for 2 to 3 minutes, flipping. Serve immediately with maple syrup, fresh fruit such as strawberries, and a dusting of powdered sugar, if desired.

2 teaspoons olive oil

1 loaf of challah bread

3 large eggs (or proportionate egg replacement of your choice)

1 vanilla bean, pod scraped

2 teaspoons pure vanilla extract

¼ teaspoon ground cinnamon

Maple syrup, for serving

Fresh fruit, for serving

1 teaspoon powdered sugar, for serving, optional

COOK'S NOTES

INTUITIVE MOMENTS

A cook is born. French toast may have been the first thing I ever truly learned to cook as a child. I started making it for myself when I was about eight years old. On some Saturday mornings, my mother would have to work. Therefore, if I wanted French toast, I needed to learn how to make it myself or I would not have it until a weekend that my mom was off. My kids now make their own French toast because they know I am not always able to be home to prepare it; plus, they are old enough to whip it up themselves.

This recipe, of course, has improved since I was a childhood cook. It's dairy free and more delicious. Any bread can be used for French toast—but all breads are not equal. Experiment with your bread. How thick or thin do you want it? Do you need to avoid gluten? Grab a loaf of gluten-free bread, which will work just as well with the ingredients in this recipe. Challah is delicious, and my body can tolerate it. Tweak and adjust this recipe to your liking and dietary needs, and you're sure to find perfection as well, so you and your family can love it and devour it.

COOK'S NOTES

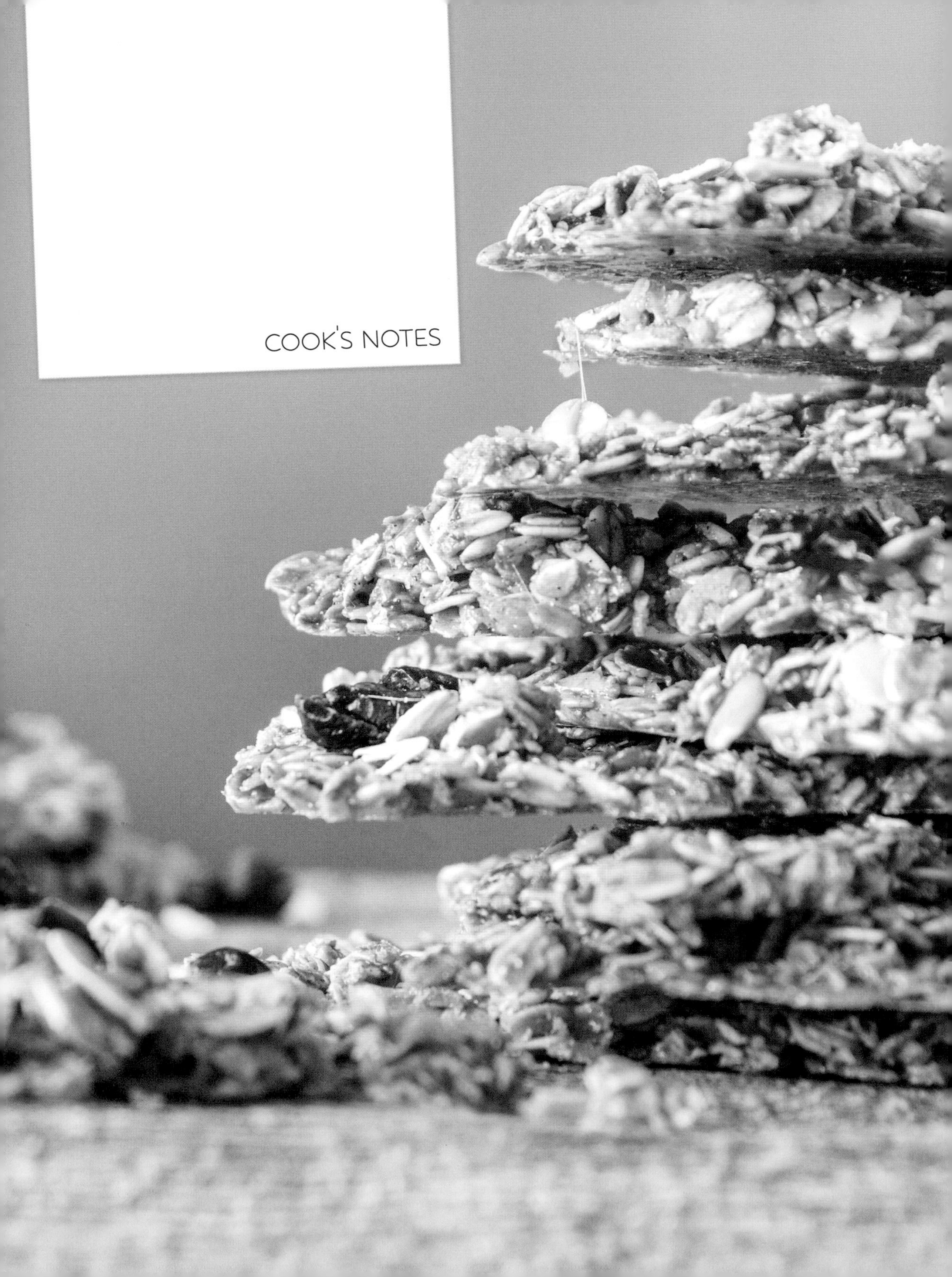

Granola Brittle ✈

SERVES 4 TO 6 This may be the most versatile recipe in this book. And, it might be the most fun to make, too. I enjoy the option of breaking this down into various pieces—small, big like granola bars, or tiny, as an addition to other recipes. My son makes his cereal out of this. Both kids enjoy it as an after-school snack. I add it to the Antioxidant Fruit Salad (recipe on page 24). And, when I am traveling by car or I have to get on a plane, I try to make this the day before and pack it so I have a great, healthy, hunger-curbing option with me.

1. Preheat oven to 350 degrees F. Line a baking sheet with parchment paper and set aside. In a large bowl, add the oats and cinnamon.

2. In a small bowl, whisk together the following wet ingredients: coconut oil, maple syrup, pure vanilla extract, and apple cider vinegar. Pour the mixture over the oats and the cinnamon, and mix together. Then add the brown rice syrup over all the ingredients to seal it, and toss until thoroughly coated.

3. Transfer the granola to a baking sheet and place in the oven for 10 minutes. At the 10-minute mark, toss the granola and transfer back to the oven to bake for an additional 10 to 12 minutes. After removing from the oven, allow the granola to cool completely without stirring; this will ensure some clusters, and you can break it up in pieces! If you like, you can make your own trail mix by crumbling the granola and mixing in raisins, dried cranberries, and/or pumpkin seeds. Enjoy as a great healthy snack.

3 cups gluten-free rolled oats

1½ teaspoons ground cinnamon

¼ cup melted coconut oil

3 tablespoons maple syrup

2 teaspoons pure vanilla extract

½ teaspoon apple cider vinegar

¾ cup brown rice syrup

½ cup raisins, optional

½ cup dried cranberries, optional

1 cup pumpkin seeds, optional

INTUITIVE MOMENTS

The name says it all. Break apart, chew, and devour.

Through trial and error my homemade granola began to resemble the form of peanut brittle—but without nuts and all the unhealthy preservatives. Once this granola brittle comes out of the oven, everyone will ask, "Oh my God, what smells so good?" They'll want to start nibbling right away, but make sure to wait for it to cool. Be careful—if it's too hot it can burn your tongue!

My family and friends love this recipe. There's almost always a bowl of granola brittle in the house—or some form of granola. It's there for healthy snacking (available so my family will reach for that instead of going to get something less healthy). I use it to add texture and flavor to my morning oatmeal. My kids and their friends grub on this all the time after school. It can be sprinkled over ice cream or added on top of the fruit salad on page 24 or 26.

You can also add your favorite extras such as blueberries or raspberries. Make it like you want it. It's fun, chewy, nutritious, and fantastically tasty!

Saturday Morning Spelt and Oat Pancakes

YIELD: 6 PANCAKES Pancakes without guilt? Indulge in these scrumptious pancakes and rest assured that you're not going to have the yucky, full feeling that many of us experience from white flour.

---

1 cup spelt flour

½ cup oat flour

1 tablespoon baking powder

¼ teaspoon baking soda

1 cup rice milk

1 tablespoon maple syrup, plus more for topping

1 tablespoon melted coconut oil, or olive oil, plus more for pan

1 teaspoon pure vanilla extract

1. In a medium bowl, whisk together the spelt flour, oat flour, baking powder, and baking soda.

2. In another medium bowl, add the rice milk, maple syrup, coconut or olive oil, and pure vanilla extract; mix until combined. Add the wet ingredients to the dry ingredients and mix just until speckles of flour disappear.

3. Heat a nonstick skillet over medium heat. Melt a little under a teaspoon of coconut oil or olive oil in the pan, and when hot, use a ¼-cup measure to scoop out mounds of batter onto the skillet. Cook on each side for 1 to 2 minutes. Repeat until you've worked your way through the remaining batter, adding more oil to the skillet as needed. Serve with a drizzle of maple syrup.

COOK'S NOTES

Huevos Rancheros (Egg or Extra-Firm Tofu) with Black Beans

SERVES 4 I personally love the heartiness of beans combined with the excitement of spice, which makes this Huevos Rancheros recipe a slam-dunk. If you do not eat eggs, guess what: Here is a tasty way you can still enjoy this fabulous ethnic dish. I personally use tofu—yes, tofu—as my egg alternative and enjoy every bite. Whether you decide to use tofu or eggs, this recipe is so delicious.

1 tomato, diced

¼ yellow onion, finely minced

Juice from 1 lime

Sea salt or Sea Veg

¼ cup soy cream cheese

1 tablespoon rice milk

1 tablespoon olive oil or coconut oil

4 large eggs or 3 ounces tofu, sliced into 4 equal squares

2 cups cooked black beans (recipe on page 55)

1 batch of guacamole (recipe on page 137)

¼ cup cilantro leaves, minced, for garnish

1. To make pico de gallo, combine tomato, onion, lime juice, and pinch of sea salt or Sea Veg. Give it a taste and adjust the salt to your liking.

2. To make the dairy-free sour cream, add the soy cream cheese and rice milk to a small bowl; whisk until smooth.

3. Set a small sauté pan over medium-high heat and add the olive oil or coconut oil. When the oil is hot, fry the eggs, one at a time, until cooked to your liking. If using tofu, add the tofu slices and cook until lightly browned, flipping halfway through, about 3 to 5 minutes on each side.

4. To assemble, divide the black beans between plates. Top each plate with a fried egg or a square of tofu, a dollop of dairy-free sour cream, a spoonful of pico de gallo, and guacamole. Garnish with cilantro.

COOK'S NOTES

INTUITIVE MOMENTS

There's nothing better than starting your day with a little kick and lot of protein. Huevos Rancheros had always been one of my favorite breakfasts. Actually, I would eat it any time throughout the day. I love the hearty black beans, the pico de gallo, and of course the avocado. But if I didn't eat eggs, would I be willing to give up one of my favorite meals? Absolutely not. It took some experimentation, but tofu, as an alternative to eggs, does the trick. It provides great texture, and it's a great source of protein to get you through your day.

With Extra-Firm Tofu

Cozy Millet and Brown Rice Porridge

SERVES 4 Millet is a good grain option to make a satisfying, nutrient-rich, hot breakfast cereal. I found this to be a great alternative for anyone who wants a hot cereal that is relatively high in protein and vitamins.

4½ cups rice milk

1 cup brown rice

½ cup millet

¼ cup maple syrup

½ teaspoon ground cinnamon

½ pint of fresh raspberries

1. In a medium pot, combine the rice milk, brown rice, millet, maple syrup, and cinnamon. Bring the mixture to a simmer, reduce the heat to low, add the raspberries, and cover the pan. Cook until the rice is almost tender, about 30 minutes.

2. At the 30-minute mark, uncover and simmer for an additional 10 to 15 minutes, until the brown rice is cooked. If at any time too much liquid has evaporated, feel free to mix in an additional ½ cup of rice milk. Lastly, the raspberries should be very soft at this point—use the back of a spoon to smash the raspberries, and then mix them back into the porridge. Divide between four bowls and serve immediately.

> ### *Did You Know?*
> *Grains are found in many foods; they're not only limited to rice, breads, cereals, and pastas.*

COOK'S NOTES

Vegetarian

Snack-Time Tofu Dip with Crudités ✈

SERVES 4 TO 6 Just because you may not consume certain foods for health reasons or health decisions does not mean you have to eliminate them all together. You can still get a great crudité by using tofu as your base instead of a dairy-based product. This dip is so delicious, guests won't even know it is not dairy!

1 (14-ounce) package firm tofu, chopped

1 tablespoon Vegenaise®

2 teaspoons soy sauce

1 teaspoon apple cider vinegar

¼ teaspoon nutritional yeast

Pinch of sea salt or Sea Veg

Carrots, celery, broccoli, radishes, crackers, for serving

1. Combine the tofu, Vegenaise, soy sauce, apple cider vinegar, nutritional yeast, and pinch of sea salt or Sea Veg in a blender. Pulse until very smooth, scraping down the sides as needed. Give it a taste and adjust the salt according to your liking.

2. Serve with an array of carrots, celery, broccoli, radishes, or crackers.

Shut Up and Listen

We are all smart individuals. We know what foods work for us and what foods will make our bodies pay for our dining decisions later. Why continue to suffer if we no longer have to? You know a heavy lunch is going to make you sleepy in the afternoon. You know fried junk foods are going to make you feel bloated or perhaps give you heartburn. Stop doing that to yourself—you deserve to feel great when you eat. Start cooking the foods that make you feel wonderful.

COOK'S NOTES

Home-Run Gazpacho

SERVES 4 This is one of those recipes that seems like it would be much more complicated than it really is. You won't know how easy it is until you try it. Of course, there are so many ways to make this famous soup, but I loved how simple this recipe was for me the first time I played around with making it. Who knew? Get in the kitchen. Get your gazpacho on! Shut up and cook!

1. In a blender, add the tomatoes, cucumber, onion, garlic, cilantro, parsley, soy sauce, apple cider vinegar, umeboshi vinegar, and sea salt or Sea Veg. Pulse two to three times. It should not be too thick and chunky, but try to keep a few chewable pieces in the mix. Give it a taste and adjust the salt according to your liking.

2. Chill for at least one hour in the refrigerator. When ready to serve, divide among bowls, drizzle a bit of olive oil into each bowl, and garnish the bowls with a bit of cilantro.

5 vine tomatoes

½ cucumber, roughly chopped

¼ yellow onion, roughly chopped

1 garlic clove, minced

1 small handful of cilantro, plus more, minced, for garnish

1 small handful of flat-leaf parsley

1 teaspoon soy sauce

1 teaspoon apple cider vinegar

1 teaspoon umeboshi vinegar

1 teaspoon sea salt or Sea Veg

COOK'S NOTES

INTUITIVE MOMENTS

Everyone makes mistakes. But then again, it's hard to call anything a mistake if you readily admit that you don't know what you're doing. And I do admit, the first time I tried making gazpacho, I had no idea what the heck I was getting into. I knew tomato was the base. But, beyond that, I just started adding ingredients that I thought I'd seen before in gazpacho.

Batch after batch my gazpacho got better. In fact, I remember one evening when we had company at the house, and I decided to serve my gazpacho because now I was really good at making it. And that was when I really made the mistake—I forgot to season it with Sea Veg. The bowls were served at each person's place setting. The soup was in the bowls, my guests were about to be seated, and there I was running around the table trying to season each individual bowl of gazpacho before the guests came to the table to sit for the meal. Whew! It was a close call. The gazpacho would have been disgustingly bland. It was such a funny TV reality-show moment!

Cauliflower Rice Salad with Green Beans and Chickpeas

SERVES 4 TO 6 Healthy is delicious! The nutrients in this salad do not take away from how fantastic it tastes. Cauliflower, although bland in color, gives this recipe a unique twist and a tremendous amount of flavor.

1½ cup dried chickpeas

1 strip kombu

1 head cauliflower, cut into florets

¼ pound green beans, ends trimmed

Zest and juice from 1 lemon

1 tablespoon olive oil

Sea salt or Sea Veg

COOK'S NOTES

1. Prep the chickpeas by pouring them in a medium bowl and covering them with about an inch of water; cover with plastic wrap and allow them to soak overnight. Drain and wash the chickpeas and add them to a medium saucepan, along with a strip of kombu, covering them once more with 2 inches of water. Boil, covered, until tender, about 45 minutes. Drain and set aside.

2. I like using a knife to chop the cauliflower florets until they are very small, with a fine consistency. Or you can use a food processor/blender and pulse until the cauliflower resembles the texture of rice. Transfer the "cauliflower rice" to a steam basket and set over a saucepan filled with about ½ inch of simmering water. Cover and steam for about 5 minutes, until just softened. Set aside.

3. Bring a medium saucepan of water to a boil. Blanch the green beans for 30 seconds to 1 minute until their color turns bright green. Remove immediately and run under cold water; then transfer to a medium bowl.

4. To the bowl with the green beans, add the reserved chickpeas, cauliflower rice, juice from 1 lemon, and olive oil. Toss until thoroughly coated. Add salt according to your liking. Garnish with the zest of the lemon.

INTUITIVE MOMENTS

My kids were away at summer camp one year, so I decided it was time for what I called Camp Erica. I wanted and desperately needed some time to focus on myself, including my physical health, my diet, and my sleep. I also really wanted to focus on eating healthy, which meant experimenting with new recipes. And that's what inspired this recipe.

I play close attention to my meals when I dine out. I look at how a dish is prepared because I know that if I love it, I'll run home to create my own healthier version. This salad is one of those. In fact, I was anxious to get home (I was staying at a hotel in another country) to my own kitchen and give this recipe a try.

Did You Know?

Eating a healthy diet can provide you with more mental clarity and focus.

Rice-Free Cauliflower Sushi Rolls ✈

YIELD: 12 CUT SUSHI ROLLS Move over rice and guilt! I seriously jumped up and down with joy when I realized I was still able to make sushi at home without any grains. Cauliflower, as a substitution for rice, will not let you down! In fact, I wish I was in the room with you right now. I promise you will experience the same shock and joy about this recipe as I did! These are sushi rolls you can feel great about.

¼ head cauliflower, cut into florets

1 teaspoon sea salt or Sea Veg (skip salt if using umeboshi paste)

2 teaspoons coconut oil or olive oil

3 ounces tempeh, sliced

2 sheets of nori, divided

2 teaspoons umeboshi paste, divided (optional)

¼ raw carrot, cut into matchsticks

½ raw cucumber, cut into matchsticks

¼ cup shoyu soy sauce or soy sauce, for dipping

Handful of micro greens, for garnish

1. I like using a knife to chop the cauliflower florets until they are very small, with a fine consistency. You can also use a food processor or blender and pulse until the cauliflower resembles the texture of rice. If you're not using umeboshi, sprinkle the cauliflower with the salt and toss. Set aside. Transfer the "cauliflower rice" to a steam basket and set over a saucepan filled with about ½ inch of simmering water. Cover and steam for about 5 minutes, until just softened. Set aside.

2. Meanwhile, in a small sauté pan set over medium heat, add the coconut oil. When the oil is hot, add the tempeh and cook until slightly browned, about 2 minutes per side.

3. Set out the sheets of nori on a cutting board. If using umeboshi paste, spread a thin layer, about 1 teaspoon, on each sheet. Divide the cauliflower rice among the nori and spread it on the first half closest to you of each of the sheets. Divide the carrots, cucumber, and tempeh between the nori sheets. Rub the top of the nori sheet with a bit of water (this will help with sealing the roll). Roll the nori tightly. Repeat with the second sheet of nori. Cut the sushi into ¾-inch pieces and serve with shoyu soy sauce. Garnish with micro greens.

NOTE: *These rolls can be made a few different ways. If you like, you can leave out the tempeh and add slices of cucumber and avocado. Or add sautéed tofu, which is a version loved by my son. If you're feeling particularly hungry, you can include the tofu, cucumber, and avocado.*

COOK'S NOTES

Did You Know?

Peanuts, tree nuts, fish and seafood, wheat, dairy, soy, and eggs are the most common foods to which people are allergic. Here's a healthy alternative for you to enjoy!

Did You Know?

Your digestive system is the core to your health (so feed it well).

Orange and Fennel Salad

SERVES 4 TO 6 I get so excited about this salad each time I make it that my enthusiasm surprises me! You'll understand why after you've tried it. The citrus juice from the orange, along with the maple dressing and the fennel, plus the extra added texture and flavor from the dried cranberries, makes this salad shockingly refreshing and ever so satisfying.

1. Clean the fennel and pat dry. Layer the thin slices of fennel on serving plate, top with orange segments and cranberries, and drizzle with dressing. Enjoy immediately or store in the refrigerator until ready to serve.

2 fennel bulbs, thinly sliced

1 orange, cut in segments

¼ cup dried cranberries

½ batch of maple cider vinaigrette (about ¼ cup of dressing) (recipe on page 113)

COOK'S NOTES

Garden Arugula Green Bean Salad

SERVES 4 TO 6 If you want fresh, you've found the right recipe! The pickled onions in this salad offer gorgeous color while the arugula and the green beans provide the greens you need to feel healthy. Top it off with the light dressing made right here at home. Lovely! Fresh! Nutritious!

PICKLED RED ONION:

1 red onion, thinly sliced

½ cup apple cider vinegar

½ cup warm water

1 tablespoon maple syrup

1½ teaspoons kosher salt

SALAD:

¼ cup quinoa, rinsed

3 tablespoons olive oil, divided

¼ pound green beans, ends trimmed

Juice from ½ lemon

Sea salt or Sea Veg

4 cups packed baby arugula, washed and dried

COOK'S NOTES

1. Add the sliced onion to a sterilized, 1-cup mason jar or glass container with an airtight lid. In a measuring cup or small bowl, add the apple cider vinegar, warm water, maple syrup, and kosher salt. Pour the mixture over the onions and allow to stand until it reaches room temperature. Secure the lid and allow to stand for at least 2 hours, ideally 1 day. Once pickled, transfer to the fridge for 5 to 7 days.

2. Bring a medium pot filled halfway with water to a boil. Place the quinoa in a fine-mesh strainer and set over the boiling water; cover with a lid and allow the quinoa to steam, about 5 to 7 minutes. Heat a small sauté pan over medium heat, add 1 tablespoon of olive oil, and pour in the quinoa (it's OK if it's still wet from the steam). Cook the quinoa until it is all toasted, occasionally shaking the pan to ensure even cooking, about 4 to 5 minutes. Transfer the crispy quinoa to a small bowl and set aside.

3. Place a medium pot of water over high heat. When the water reaches a gentle boil, add the green beans and cook for 1 to 2 minutes. Drain, and immediately run cold water over the green beans to stop the cooking. Set aside.

4. In a small bowl, whisk together the remaining olive oil, lemon juice, and Sea Veg or sea salt. In a large serving bowl, add the arugula, the green beans, and ½ cup of pickled onion; pour in the dressing and toss the arugula, beans, and onion until the leaves are thoroughly coated. Garnish with the quinoa crumbs.

Did You Know?

You can get calcium from sources other than dairy—for example, from your green leafy vegetables.

New York Bowl ✈

SERVES 1 Quinoa has been such a beneficial ingredient in my home since I discovered it years ago! This seed, which we sometimes mistake as a grain, offers a full source of protein and fiber that is wonderfully nutritious. Even if quinoa is new to you, I beg you to try it because it may soon become a staple in your kitchen as well. My kids and friends never get tired of it.

1. In a medium saucepan set over medium heat, combine the quinoa and the water. Bring to a simmer, cover, and reduce the heat to medium low, allowing it to cook until bloomed, about 15 minutes.

2. Add 1 tablespoon of olive oil or coconut oil to a sauté pan set over medium heat. When hot, add the tempeh and cook until light golden brown, about 1 to 2 minutes, flipping the slices halfway through. Add the artichoke hearts and peas; cook until warmed, about 2 minutes. Pour in the remaining 1 tablespoon oil and the balsamic vinegar, and cook for an additional 30 seconds, just until warmed.

3. To toast pumpkin seeds, add the dry seeds to a small skillet set over medium heat and cook, shaking the pan every so often to ensure even toasting. Stir the toasted pumpkin seeds into the other ingredients in the sauté pan and toss once more. Lastly, add the cooked quinoa and toss again. Serve immediately.

If you'd like to add more heft to this bowl, add a piece of cooked salmon or tofu— get creative. This dish is also a great place to use up sautéed vegetables.

½ cup quinoa, rinsed

1 cup water

2 tablespoons olive oil or coconut oil, divided

3 ounces tempeh, sliced

⅓ cup artichoke hearts (from a jar, packed in water)

⅓ cup frozen green peas

1 tablespoon balsamic vinegar

1 tablespoon pumpkin seeds

COOK'S NOTES

INTUITIVE MOMENTS

Inspired by hunger, some leftover quinoa, and a refrigerator full of fresh vegetables, my New York Bowl has become my go-to recipe when I want to create a quick lunch. This is the perfect dish to get some greens and satisfy any appetite without the rice. In fact, you'll notice that the quinoa in this recipe is not only more nutritious than rice, it also takes on the flavors of the other ingredients better than rice and leaves you feeling satisfied longer.

The Hollywood Bowl ✈

SERVES 1 Watch out, my friends, because after you make this recipe just a few times, you'll start to crave it. I seriously think I make this dish more often than anything else because it is so loaded with nutrients and it looks, and tastes, like health in a bowl. I love making it when my friends come to my house to eat, because no matter for whom I make it, they are surprised each time that something so healthy can taste so incredible. The arame is loaded with nutrients such as minerals and vitamins since it is a sea vegetable. I love, love, love this recipe. My Hollywood friends flip over this recipe, so the title was inspired by them!

¼ cup arame

1 cup cold water

½ cup quinoa, rinsed

1 cup water

2 tablespoons olive oil or coconut oil

½ medium carrot, grated

3 ounces firm tempeh, sliced or cubed

3 leaves of kale, stems removed and leaves torn

1 garlic clove, minced

1 tablespoon fresh lemon juice, plus more for finish

¼ large avocado, sliced

1. In a small bowl, soak the arame in 1 cup of cold water for 10 minutes, until slightly softened. Drain and set aside.

2. In a medium saucepan set over medium-high heat, add the quinoa and water; bring to a gentle boil, reduce the heat to a simmer, cover with a lid, and cook for 15 minutes, until the quinoa has bloomed and the water has evaporated. Set aside.

3. In a large sauté pan set over medium heat, pour in the olive oil or coconut oil. When the oil is hot, add the grated carrot and tempeh. Cook for about 2 minutes, until the tempeh is lightly browned and the carrots have softened slightly.

4. Add the kale and cook for 2 additional minutes, until bright green and slightly wilted. Mix in the garlic and cook until fragrant, about 1 minute. Squeeze in the lemon juice, and add the arame and cooked quinoa. Toss everything together one last time. Top with the sliced avocado. If you like, you can squeeze a quarter of a lemon over the top for some added freshness.

COOK'S NOTES

Did You Know?

Some foods can make you feel heavy, bloated, yucky, and distracted, but not this yummy, healthy, vibrant bowl.

Backyard Pickled Vegetables ✈

I know this may sound southern or country to ya'll, but do not let the word "pickled" fool you. This recipe is not only pretty and colorful, the taste is awesome! It is so easy to make, and it definitely adds a little something extra to a number of your other favorite recipes in *Shut Up and Cook*, especially some of the salads.

1. In a 2-cup mason jar or glass container with an airtight lid, add one of the vegetables (carrots, radishes, or cauliflower) listed at left. In a small bowl, mix together the apple cider vinegar, warm water, maple syrup, and kosher salt; stir until everything is thoroughly combined. Pour the pickling liquid over the vegetables and secure the lid. Allow to stand for 1 day for a light pickling or up to 3 days for a strong pickling.

FOR SERVING: *These pickles are simply delicious on their own. They're also wonderful when tossed into a summer salad or even drizzled with a bit of olive oil.*

COOK'S NOTES

PICKLED CARROTS:

2 medium carrots, cut into matchsticks

1 cup apple cider vinegar

½ cup warm water

3 tablespoons maple syrup

1 tablespoon kosher salt

PICKLED RADISHES:

5 to 7 radishes, trimmed and quartered

1 cup apple cider vinegar

½ cup warm water

3 tablespoons maple syrup

1 tablespoon kosher salt

PICKLED CAULIFLOWER:

½ head of cauliflower, florets trimmed

1 cup apple cider vinegar

½ cup warm water

2 tablespoons maple syrup

1 tablespoon kosher salt

Load 'em Up Vegetable Stir-Fry

SERVES 4 It's a struggle for most households—I simply cannot seem to get enough servings of vegetables in my family's daily diet. However, like any food, vegetables with great flavor don't create complaints; they elicit compliments—even from kids. This dish is not loaded with anything other than love and wonderful, colorful, nutritious and delicious vegetables. You decide whether to eat this by itself or over noodles. I find vermicelli to be a light, nice mix with vegetables.

8 ounces rice
vermicelli noodles

3 cups boiling water

2 tablespoons olive oil

1 leek, pale green and
white parts, thinly
sliced vertically

1-inch knob ginger,
finely grated

1 garlic clove, minced

¼ head of broccoli,
florets trimmed

¼ head of cauliflower,
florets trimmed

1 carrot, peeled and sliced

4 dried sliced lotus
root, rinsed (optional)

3 tablespoons low-
sodium soy sauce

½ bunch of kale, washed

1. Add the vermicelli noodles to a bowl. Pour the boiling water over the noodles, stirring every so often with a fork, and allow to stand for about 1 to 3 minutes or per your package's instructions. Drain the noodles and set aside.

2. In a sauté pan set over medium heat, add the olive oil. When the oil is hot, add the leek and cook until softened, about 2 minutes. Next, stir in the ginger and garlic; give it a toss and add the broccoli, cauliflower, carrot, and lotus root, if using, cooking for about 5 minutes, until the vegetables are slightly softened and bright in color. Pour in the soy sauce and add the kale; cover the pan and cook for an additional 3 to 5 minutes, until the kale is bright in color and slightly wilted. Add the cooked noodles to the stir-fry mixture and toss, adding a splash more soy sauce if you like. Don't be shy to grab a fork and really get in there so everything is thoroughly mixed together. Divide among the bowls and serve immediately.

COOK'S NOTES

INTUITIVE MOMENTS

The kids—they were ravenous. The clock—well, it wasn't giving me enough time to get ready and prepare something worthy of being called a meal . . . or so I thought. In a panic, I dashed into the kitchen, grabbed all the vegetables I could find, drizzled some olive oil in the pan, and ironically created a dish they still enjoy today. This vegetable stir-fry lets my kids get their grub on! They dig in. They gobble it up, and it keeps them full and happy. Serve these nutritious veggies over some brown rice or quinoa and your family will not only leave the table with satisfied appetites and smiles on their faces, but also with the vitamins and minerals their bodies need for good health.

Harvest Acorn Squash with Cinnamon Maple Syrup

SERVES 2 Do you remember the foods you hated as a child? I detested squash growing up. The smell, texture—everything about it. But all that changed when I discovered a way to cook it that actually tasted fantastic. And, because I didn't like squash as a kid, I was dumbfounded the first time I saw my own kids eat this dish—and enjoy it—before they were even teenagers.

1 (2-pound) acorn squash, halved and seeds scooped out

1 tablespoon nondairy butter

2 teaspoons maple syrup

½ teaspoon ground cinnamon

Pinch of nutmeg

1. Preheat oven to 400 degrees F. Line a baking sheet with parchment paper and set aside.

2. Place the halved acorn squash, cut side up, on the baking sheet. In a small saucepan set over low heat, melt the nondairy butter. Stir in the maple syrup, cinnamon, and nutmeg. Generously brush the flesh of the acorn squash with the maple syrup mixture and transfer to the oven to roast for 40 to 50 minutes, until completely tender when poked with a fork.

Shut Up and Listen

I created these recipes with one thing in mind: health. Health is wellness, and it is the most important thing you can have, as you only get one life. This is the power of eating nutritionally. I've personally seen and suffered the effects of eating unhealthfully—and trust me, I ate and grubbed and had my moments of unhealthy indulgence—but I realized it was no longer helping me at all. It was working against me, not for me. Now I've reaped the benefits of eating healthy foods and feeding my loved ones in the same way. I would never go back.

COOK'S NOTES

Yum-Yum Black Beans

SERVES 4 TO 6 Simple meals can also be the ones that you and your family, friends, and guests will rave about the most. Why? Because when you get creative with simplicity, you often concoct recipes that become 100 percent your own. I like to experiment with dried beans to add extra protein and real satisfaction to serve up some wonderful meals. I think I make these tasty black beans at least once a week.

1. In a medium bowl, add the black beans and cover with about 3 inches of water. Cover the bowl and allow to soak on the kitchen counter for at least 4 hours, ideally overnight.

2. Drain the beans and transfer to a large pot, along with the strip of kombu, minced onion, and enough water so the beans' surface is covered by about 3 inches. Bring the mixture to a boil and then immediately reduce the heat so it simmers. Cover the pot and cook the beans for about 1 hour, until slightly softened. Uncover the pot and cook for an additional 20 to 30 minutes, until tender and some of the water has reduced. Drain the beans and transfer to the refrigerator to cool.

NOTE: *I also love to add a handful of sautéed minced cilantro and a few sautéed cloves of garlic for added flavor.*

2 cups dried black beans

1 strip kombu

½ yellow onion, finely minced

COOK'S NOTES

COOK'S NOTES

Mother Earth Collard Green Wraps ✈

YIELD: 10 TO 12 WRAPS Collard greens were always that farm-to-table staple food for my ninety-three-year-young Nana in her day. She would go in her family garden to get them, clean them, and eat them. This leafy vegetable only does the body good—there are no negatives! Being loaded with those micronutrients—minerals and vitamins—is the reason I always buy them and keep them in my medicine cabinet (my refrigerator). I love experimenting and making different recipes with collard greens. This mixture is great for anyone craving a leafy vegetable with a few extra vegetables, and it's a fun way to eat these beautiful leaves.

1. Place the vermicelli noodles in a medium bowl. Cover the noodles with boiling water and allow to stand for about 3 minutes, until the noodles are tender. Drain the noodles and rinse with cold water. Transfer to a small bowl. Toss the noodles with the olive oil, lemon juice, and sea salt or Sea Veg. Set aside.

2. Prep the collard green leaves by running your knife along each side of the stem, removing it from the center. Each collard green leaf should give you two wraps. Repeat with the remaining collard green leaves. Place a small handful of vermicelli noodles on the third of the leaf closest to you. Top with a few pieces of carrot, cucumber, and a sliver of avocado. Roll the collard green leaf half tightly and transfer to a serving plate. Repeat the filling and rolling step with the remaining collard green leaves. You should end up with about 10 to 12 collard green wraps, depending on the size of the leaves.

3 ounces rice vermicelli noodles

3 cups boiling water

1 teaspoon olive oil

2 teaspoons lemon juice (from ½ lemon)

¼ teaspoon sea salt or Sea Veg

5 to 6 raw collard green leaves, washed thoroughly and patted dry

½ raw carrot, cut into small matchsticks

½ raw cucumber, cut into small matchsticks

1 avocado, peeled and thinly sliced

INTUITIVE MOMENTS

It was a holiday. Of course, I love nothing more than filling my home with extended family and extra friends to celebrate. And this recipe was inspired by a close friend of mine, who actually rejected my invitation. How rude, right? Well, she was attempting to be polite because she was eating a raw-food diet at the time and didn't want to impose her dietary restrictions on my holiday cooking. That's understandable, but I wasn't going to stand for it. She was coming. I was cooking, and I told her, "I got this. I got you covered."

To my surprise, my first attempt at cooking a raw-food meal was a raging success. My friend loved it. And in the process I created something that I've made for my friends and myself ever since. Of course, you can create your own variations on this recipe. You'll notice that the recipe includes noodles. But if you want to go raw like my friend, skip the noodles.

Zucchini and Carrot Pasta

SERVES 4 There's magic in pasta. You know it. I know it. But we also know there's guilt in pasta. With this guilt-free and delicious recipe, you can now enjoy a creative way of feeling like you're eating pasta without the bloat, or the hour nap after you clean your plate. Vegetables, surprisingly, make a healthy, flavorful, almost-too-good-to-be-true substitution for grain pasta.

Olive oil

1 garlic clove, minced

2 cups store-bought marinara sauce (I like a good organic jar of marinara sauce)

¼ cup fresh cilantro, minced

¼ cup flat-leaf Italian parsley, minced

Sea salt or Sea Veg

2 teaspoons soy sauce

2 medium green zucchini

2 medium yellow zucchini

2 medium carrots

1. In a medium saucepan set over medium heat, add a teaspoon of olive oil. When the oil is hot, add the minced garlic and cook until softened, about 1 minute. Pour in the marinara sauce, along with the cilantro, parsley, pinch of Sea Veg or sea salt, and soy sauce. Bring the sauce to a gentle boil and allow to cook for about 10 minutes while you make the rest of the dish.

2. Using a vegetable peeler or a mandoline, peel thin ribbons of the zucchini and carrots, lengthwise, end to end.

3. Heat a tablespoon of olive oil in a medium pan over medium heat. Add the zucchini and carrot noodles and a little sea salt or Sea Veg. Cook for about 1 to 3 minutes, depending on how crunchy you like the zucchini and carrot noodles to be. Divide the noodles among the plates. Spoon sauce over each bed of noodles.

COOK'S NOTES

INTUITIVE MOMENTS

For the love of pasta, why does it have to be pasta? Adored globally, pasta is a standard in many recipes. But, it's also known for high levels of carbohydrates (some marathon runners eat it for fuel before a big race). I had heard how people were using vegetables as pasta, but I was curious how they were preparing these to actually taste good. Knowing that I wasn't a professional chef, I decided it would be interesting to see how the pros did it. During Camp Erica, I asked a chef to prepare vegetable pasta. Honestly, I never thought I would love this because I had never been a fan of zucchini. Some may say or think that I'm a picky eater. I didn't like it cubed or thick, or any other way for that matter. Boy, did I change my mind when the chef prepared it for me. It was beautiful— thinly sliced and the texture was perfect. I studied it, tasted it, loved it, and then went home to try making it for myself.

It's hard to imagine that anything can replace regular pasta. But you'll be shocked by just how delicious these "noodles" can be. Cover them with marinara sauce. You could even pair this with your turkey meatballs on page 81 for an Italian feast without the guilt, or the food coma that often follows a typical pasta plate. I cannot get enough of this—it is so light and yummy to the tummy.

Soul-Warming Black-Eyed Peas

SERVES 4 TO 6 Protein, fiber, and a satisfied soul, this recipe will have you saying "yum yum yum." Black-eyed peas are not just for welcoming in the new year as some people believe. This recipe is a winner year-round.

1. In a medium bowl, add the black-eyed peas and cover with 3 cups of water. Cover the bowl with plastic wrap or top with a plate and allow to soak on your kitchen counter for at least 4 hours, ideally overnight.

2. The next day, drain the black-eyed peas and rinse under cold water. Add them to a medium pot, along with the chopped onion, apple cider vinegar, strip of kombu, and enough water so the black-eyed peas' surface is covered by about 3 inches. Bring the mixture to a boil, and then reduce the heat to a simmer. Cover the pot and cook until the beans are tender, about 1 hour. Mix in about a teaspoon of sea salt or Sea Veg; give it a taste and adjust the salt accordingly.

1 cup dried black-eyed peas

3 cups water

¼ yellow onion, finely chopped

1 teaspoon apple cider vinegar

1 strip kombu

Sea salt or Sea Veg

COOK'S NOTES

INTUITIVE MOMENTS

I seriously don't remember a Thanksgiving Dinner without black-eyed peas—as a little girl, as an adult, or as a mother myself. In fact, I don't think I remember too many holiday meals without them. They were a staple and a standard. And, I don't know if it's true, but superstition says they are lucky. In fact, in the South, many people eat black-eyed peas at New Year's celebrations. It's not clear why this has become a tradition. Some say it dates back to the Civil War. Others say it dates all the way back to ancient Egypt, when it was supposedly believed that eating a meager food like black-eyed peas revealed that a person showed humility toward the gods. Personally, I don't eat them for luck. I don't eat them for tradition. I make them because I love them. I eat black-eyed peas because they're delicious and provide a great source of fiber. If they also happen to be lucky, well, I'll take that, too.

Black Bean Mango Salad with a Kick

SERVES 4 TO 6 Sometimes the ingredients you think won't work together turn out to create absolute magic. This is that magic recipe of strange combinations. It's sweet and spicy at the same time. Plus, I just cannot say it enough, the black bean is one of my favorites because it provides a substantial amount of protein.

1 tablespoon olive oil

1 tablespoon cilantro, minced, plus extra leaves for garnish

1 teaspoon sea salt or Sea Veg

½ teaspoon ground cumin

Pinch of chili powder

Pinch of ground cayenne pepper

Juice from 1 lemon

Juice from ½ lime

2 cups cooked black beans (recipe on page 55)

1 mango, diced

¼ red onion, finely minced

½ avocado, pitted, peeled, and finely diced

1. In a medium bowl, whisk together the olive oil, minced cilantro, sea salt or Sea Veg, cumin, chili powder, cayenne pepper, lemon juice, and lime juice. Add the black beans, mango, and red onion; toss the salad together until the mixture is thoroughly combined. Lastly, just before serving, gently fold in the diced avocado. Serve immediately or you can let it chill in the refrigerator for about 30 minutes to an hour. Garnish with a few cilantro leaves.

COOK'S NOTES

INTUITIVE MOMENTS

Children often don't like food to touch other food on their plate. The vegetables go on the left. The protein goes on the right. And, maybe, if there's enough space to include a third option on the plate, you can squeeze it in at the top or the bottom. It's common in picky eaters. And, it described my eating habits when I was a kid—nothing could touch or it somehow was ruined.

That all changed the day my mother introduced me to this Black Bean Mango Salad. Somehow the flavors bounced off each other and complemented each other amazingly well. My mother made this without the mango. I decided to be a bit fancy and add mango to see what I could achieve.

This is a great dish that your family and friends will enjoy. Try it tonight.

Did You Know?

You can get protein from sources other than animal products—for instance, from beans.

Coconut Rice

SERVES 4 Let's never be boring when we're trying to cook healthier. If I am going to eat rice (this recipe is a great example), I like to doctor it up a bit by adding something gentle and yummy to it, so it is not so plain—not so boring. Coconut milk does exactly that to this dish.

1 cup brown jasmine rice

1 cup light coconut milk

1 cup water

½ teaspoon sea salt or Sea Veg

2 tablespoons cilantro, minced

Did You Know?

Foods packed in aluminum cans may be linked to certain health issues. Some experts say aluminum can lead to Alzheimer's disease.

1. Add the brown rice to a strainer and rinse under cold water. Drain and then pour into a medium pot set over medium heat; add the coconut milk, water, and sea salt or Sea Veg. Bring the mixture to a boil and immediately reduce the heat to low, covering the pan. Cook for about 20 minutes, until the rice is tender and the liquid has completely evaporated.

2. Turn off the heat and allow the mixture to stand, covered, for an additional 5 minutes. Uncover the pot and mix in the minced cilantro. Give it a taste and adjust the salt according to your preference.

COOK'S NOTES

Kelp Noodle Stir-Fry ✈

SERVES 2 Kelp is a sea vegetable that is very high in minerals and also a great source of iodine, which is why I like to eat kelp noodles. I enjoy mixing it with a bit of heat and these scrumptious easy vegetables.

1. Add the olive oil to a large sauté pan set over medium heat. When the oil is hot, add the cauliflower and broccoli and cook until slightly softened, about 3 minutes.

2. Next, add the carrots and tempeh and cook for an additional 2 minutes. Pour in the frozen peas, kale, kelp noodles, soy sauce, and water.

3. Toss the entire mixture together, cooking everything until the peas and kale turn a bright green and the kelp noodles have softened slightly, about 3 minutes. Divide between bowls and garnish with micro greens.

2 tablespoon olive oil or coconut oil

1 cup cauliflower florets (from about ½ head of cauliflower)

½ cup broccoli florets (from about ¼ head of broccoli)

1 cup carrots, diced (from 2 carrots)

8 ounces tempeh, cubed

⅔ cup frozen peas

1 cup packed kale leaves

8 ounces kelp noodles, rinsed and drained

¼ cup shoyu soy sauce

¼ cup water

Handful of micro greens, for garnish

Shut Up and Listen

What I learned from healthy eating is that nature is medicine. That is why I have to share this vital information with you. You'd better believe that I once ate the types of foods tested in a lab, which were altered to taste a certain way and created more like science projects. But that wasn't good for my body—it wasn't natural medicine. It was the opposite. Be mindful of your medicine. Use nature to your advantage.

COOK'S NOTES

Avocado Carrot Salad ✈

SERVES 4 I admit, I am no Chef Jean-Georges Vongerichten by any means, but I am a fan of this salad that he serves at one of his famous restaurants: ABC Kitchen. Of course, I do not have his recipe, so I decided to craft my own for friends and loved ones.

1. Preheat oven to 400 degrees F and line a baking sheet with parchment paper.

2. In a small bowl, whisk together the maple syrup, orange juice, lemon juice, olive oil, apple cider vinegar, ground cumin, ground cardamom, the cardamom seeds, and a few pinches of sea salt or Sea Veg. Spread the carrots out onto the baking sheet. Set 2 tablespoons of the dressing aside (we're going to add a bit more at the very end). Toss the carrots with the dressing and transfer to the oven to roast until the carrots are a bit soft or tender—about 35 to 40 minutes.

3. Transfer the roasted carrots to a serving dish. Top with diced avocado, cilantro, and micro greens; lastly, pour the reserved dressing over top.

1 teaspoon maple syrup

Juice from 1 navel orange

Juice from 1 lemon

2 tablespoons olive oil

½ teaspoon apple cider vinegar

2 teaspoons ground cumin

Generous pinch of ground cardamom

1 teaspoon cardamom seeds

Pinch of sea salt or Sea Veg

1 bunch of carrots, ends trimmed

1 avocado, pitted, peeled, and diced

1 handful of cilantro leaves, chopped, for garnish

1 handful of micro greens, for garnish

COOK'S NOTES

Fry-Free Veggie Spring Rolls ✈

YIELD: 4 ROLLS Fried foods are delicious. But if you want to improve your health, they're typically the first items on the menu that are off-limits. That doesn't mean you can't make some of your favorite things "fry-free." I, for example, had no idea that I can eat, much less make, a veggie roll without frying it. Oh my gosh, these unfried rice wraps are beyond delicious. They are so light and refreshing. The cilantro and fresh mint I add give them a taste that is just perfect.

---

1 teaspoon olive oil

4 ounces extra-firm tofu, drained, cut into ½-inch slices

Pinch of sea salt or Sea Veg

4 cups hot water

4 brown rice spring-roll wrappers

½ carrot, julienned

1 cucumber, julienned

¼ cup fresh cilantro leaves

¼ cup fresh mint leaves

½ head of purple cabbage, shredded

Soy sauce, for serving

Plum sauce (recipe on page 114), for serving

Handful of mint leaves, for garnish

1. Heat the olive oil in a small sauté pan set over medium-high heat. Sprinkle the tofu with the sea salt or Sea Veg. Add the tofu and cook on each side for about 1 to 2 minutes, until lightly browned. Transfer to a cutting board until assembly time.

2. In a large bowl, add about 4 cups of hot water. Dip the spring-roll wrapper into the water, moving it around a bit, until it softens. Transfer the wrapper to a cutting board and lay it flat. To the center of the wrapper, add two pieces of tofu and a few pieces of carrot and cucumber, a few cilantro leaves, a couple of mint leaves, and a small handful of shredded cabbage. Wrap the spring roll by folding in the sides and then rolling it like you would a burrito. Repeat with the remaining roll wrappers and filling. Serve these rolls with soy sauce or the plum sauce recipe on page 114, and garnish with mint leaves.

COOK'S NOTES

Black Bean Burgers

SERVES 4 Don't knock it until you try it. Packed with protein and veggies, this recipe is not only healthy for you, but something you can indulge in freely with all your favorite burger toppings.

1 tablespoon plus
¼ cup olive oil

½ cup thinly sliced
leek (from ½ leek)

1 garlic clove, minced

2 cups cooked black beans
(recipe on page 55) or
prepackaged black beans

1 tablespoon fresh
cilantro, minced

1 tablespoon fresh
Italian parsley, minced

½ teaspoon apple
cider vinegar

1 teaspoon umeboshi
vinegar

¼ cup gluten-free and
dairy-free bread crumbs

½ teaspoon sea salt
or Sea Veg

1. Preheat oven to 350 degrees F. Line a baking sheet with parchment paper. In a small sauté pan set over medium-low heat, add a tablespoon of olive oil. When hot, add the leeks and garlic clove; cook until softened and translucent, about 5 minutes.

2. Transfer the softened leeks and garlic to a large bowl, along with the cooked black beans, minced cilantro, Italian parsley, apple cider vinegar, umeboshi vinegar, remaining ¼ cup olive oil, bread crumbs, and sea salt or Sea Veg. Using a fork, mash the black beans until they're mostly broken up but some whole beans are still visible. Give the mixture a good stir, being sure all of the ingredients are evenly incorporated.

3. Divide the black bean mixture into quarters and form them into ¾-inch thick patties. Transfer the patties to the baking sheet and place in the oven to bake for 15 to 20 minutes, until warmed all the way through.

Did You Know?

When I was pregnant, I thought I had to eat cheese and chicken to get calcium and protein. I was wrong.

COOK'S NOTES

Canada Cauliflower

YIELD: 1 CAULIFLOWER HEAD Simple as simple gets. The vegetable we can never get enough of: cauliflower. I call this Canada Cauliflower because I got the idea for this dish while visiting friends in Canada. They were cooking it in their oven, which inspired me to make it myself at home.

1 full head of cauliflower

2 teaspoons olive oil

1. Rinse the head of cauliflower in cold water and pat dry.

2. You are going to bake the cauliflower whole so do not chop up it up. Remove only the green leaves.

3. Preheat oven to 375 degrees F. Place the raw cauliflower on the top rack of your oven. Yes, place it bare on your oven's rack—don't be afraid. Allow to bake and toast for about 40 minutes. You want it to get a nice tan all around. Remove from your oven and then cut up into pieces. You can drizzle olive oil around the cauliflower and then serve.

COOK'S NOTES

Tofu Veggie Burritos ✈

SERVES 4 Kudos to the person who invented the burrito. She or he definitely gave the world one of our favorite wraps. However, burritos don't necessarily need animal protein to be tasty. Tofu, seasoned properly, is a fantastic substitute for beef, chicken, or pork. The texture is amazing. The flavor is amazing. And the health benefits, well, they're amazing, too!

2 teaspoons plus one tablespoon olive oil

½ cup brown rice or quinoa, rinsed under cold water

½ cup of water

Pinch sea salt or Sea Veg

1 medium carrot, diced

1 cup broccoli florets (from about ¼ stalk of broccoli)

6 ounces crumbled tofu

1 cup packed kale leaves

½ teaspoon turmeric powder

½ teaspoon chipotle powder

2 tablespoons cilantro, minced

4 gluten-free brown rice tortillas, or your choice of tortillas, for serving

1. In a small saucepan set over medium heat, add 2 teaspoons olive oil. When the oil is hot, add the brown rice or quinoa. Pour in ½ cup of water and a pinch of sea salt or Sea Veg. Bring the water to a simmer and then immediately turn the heat down to low. Cover the pot and cook for about 10 to 12 minutes, until the quinoa or brown rice has bloomed and the water has evaporated. Set aside.

2. In a medium sauté pan set over medium heat, add the remaining tablespoon of olive oil. When the oil is hot, add the carrot and cook until slightly softened, about 2 minutes. Next, add the broccoli florets, crumbled tofu, kale, turmeric powder, chipotle powder, and a few pinches of sea salt or Sea Veg. Toss the mixture together and cook for about 2 to 3 minutes, until the broccoli and kale turn bright green. Mix in the minced cilantro, and then divide the filling among the tortillas. Top with a liberal spoonful of rice or quinoa. Fold in the sides of each of the tortillas and then fold the tortilla over the filling, forming burritos.

Did You Know?

Turmeric is a spice that's known to reduce swelling and inflammation inside our body.

COOK'S NOTES

Poultry

City Jerk Chicken

SERVES 4 Let faraway places inspire your cooking creativity. I do. It keeps cooking interesting. I like bringing a bit of island feel into my home by preparing this jerk poultry for friends and family, especially as a surprise. Because, let's be honest— when was the last time you showed up at someone's home and they offered you jerk chicken? It's fun and adventurous.

---

2 pounds bone-in chicken thighs and drumsticks

½ cup white distilled vinegar

Juice from 1 lime

1 tablespoon apple cider vinegar

1 tablespoon fresh minced cilantro

2 scallions, thinly sliced

2 teaspoons ground allspice

2 teaspoons ground cayenne pepper, depending on your spice tolerance

1 teaspoon sea salt or Sea Veg

1 teaspoon garlic powder

1 teaspoon red chili flakes

½ teaspoon ground chili powder

½ teaspoon ground cumin

2 tablespoons olive oil

1. Rinse the chicken in cold water. Place the chicken in a bowl and add the vinegar. Add cold water until the liquid covers the chicken, and let sit for 10 to15 minutes. Pour off the vinegar water, and wash the chicken completely in cold water and pat dry.

2. In a large clean bowl, whisk together the lime juice, apple cider vinegar, cilantro, scallions, allspice, cayenne, sea salt or Sea Veg, garlic powder, chili flakes, chili powder, and cumin. Add the drumsticks and thighs, and toss until all the chicken is evenly coated in the marinade. Cover the bowl with plastic wrap or transfer all the seasoned chicken to a large freezer-safe bag and seal it. Then transfer to the fridge to marinate overnight.

3. Preheat oven to 275 degrees F. In a large sauté pan set over medium-high heat, pour in the olive oil. Add the drumsticks and thighs; sear on both sides for about 1 to 2 minutes until light golden brown. Transfer the chicken to a parchment-lined baking sheet and bake for 40 to 45 minutes, until crispy and browned.

COOK'S NOTES

Turkey Tacos

SERVES 4 Why not? Tacos are always a hit.

1. In a medium sauté pan or cast-iron skillet (I like to use the skillet) set over medium heat, add the olive oil. When the oil is hot, add the minced yellow onion and garlic clove, stirring frequently until softened, about 3 minutes. Next, add the ground turkey and break it up into crumbles using a wooden spoon or spatula. Mix in the tomato paste, water, cilantro, apple cider vinegar, chipotle powder, poultry seasoning, sea salt or Sea Veg, and turmeric. Cook the turkey taco mixture thoroughly, until no pink is visible.

2. Divide the taco meat between the tortillas or hard shells. Top with minced cilantro, avocado, cheese, and a few tablespoons of salsa.

TURKEY TACO MEAT:

1 tablespoon olive oil

¼ cup minced yellow onion (from ¼ onion)

1 garlic clove, minced

1 pound ground turkey

¼ cup tomato paste

1 tablespoon water

2 tablespoons fresh cilantro, minced

1 teaspoon apple cider vinegar

1 teaspoon chipotle powder

½ teaspoon poultry seasoning

½ teaspoon sea salt or Sea Veg

Pinch of turmeric

TO SERVE:

Gluten-free tortillas (or tortillas of your choice) or hard-shell tacos

¼ cup fresh cilantro, minced

1 avocado, pitted, peeled, and diced

½ cup shredded nondairy cheese or your cheese of choice

½ cup salsa (recipe on page 141)

COOK'S NOTES

INTUITIVE MOMENTS

There's serious magic in tacos. I can't explain it. Kids love them. Adults love them. I grew up eating turkey tacos and today I'd like to think that I'm just making them for my kids. But let's be honest: Taco night is for everyone. Serve them with beans and rice. The wonderful thing about tacos is that you and everyone at the table can get creative with toppings—everyone can control their own spice, size, and creations. In addition to the toppings, tacos have a special filling: enthusiasm! Say the word "tacos" to your family tonight and, just like mine, they'll probably flock to the dinner table.

Bun-less Turkey Burgers

SERVES 4 Who needs a bun when lettuce can work just as well and offer better health benefits? These bun-less burgers are great for high-protein, low-carb eaters.

1. In a large bowl, mix together the ground turkey, soy sauce, apple cider vinegar, cilantro, parsley, garlic powder, Italian seasoning, and sea salt or Sea Veg. Scoop out 2 heaping tablespoons at a time to form into 4 individual patties.

2. In a medium sauté pan set over medium-high heat, pour in the olive oil. When the oil is hot, add the turkey burger patties and cook on each side for 3 to 4 minutes, until firm to the touch. Of course you can still serve these patties in between buns, but my favorite route is to serve each one on a leaf of lettuce with a slice of tomato.

1 pound ground turkey

2 teaspoons soy sauce

½ teaspoon apple cider vinegar

1 tablespoon fresh cilantro, minced

1 tablespoon fresh flat-leaf parsley, minced

¼ teaspoon garlic powder

¼ teaspoon dried Italian seasoning

¼ teaspoon sea salt or Sea Veg

2 tablespoons olive oil

4 leaves of lettuce, for serving

1 tomato, sliced, for serving

COOK'S NOTES

INTUITIVE MOMENTS

Somehow, my mom was ahead of her time. I grew up eating turkey burgers, even though all my friends were eating beef. Today, of course, ground turkey is readily available at most grocery stores. But it wasn't so popular when I was kid.

My mother was also ahead of her time by making burgers without buns. When I was in middle school, she started wrapping our turkey burgers in lettuce. At first, my sisters and I looked at it and thought, "What the heck is this?" But after just a few bites, we were shocked and amazed at just how good bun-less burgers can be. When I prepare turkey burgers, I sometimes wrap them in lettuce and other times go without the lettuce. Add your favorite burger toppings and enjoy!

Mama's Turkey Meatballs

YIELD: 18 MEATBALLS Who has never eaten a turkey meatball? Surprisingly, a lot of people haven't, simply because it's difficult to find turkey meatballs in restaurants. And those frozen turkey meatballs you find at the grocery store? We can do better than that. If you've never had a turkey meatball—or never had a *great* turkey meatball—let's change that now. Shut up and cook.

1. Preheat oven to 350 degrees F. In a medium bowl, add the ground turkey, parsley, cilantro, garlic, soy sauce, apple cider vinegar, dried Italian seasoning, and sea salt or Sea Veg. Mix the ground turkey mixture until all of the ingredients are evenly distributed throughout. Scoop out a heaping tablespoon of the mixture and roll it between your palm, forming a ball. Repeat with the remaining ground turkey mixture until you have about 18 meatballs. Drizzle the olive oil in a cast-iron skillet or an oven-safe dish; transfer the meatballs to the skillet or dish. Set aside.

2. In a medium pot over medium heat, mix the jarred marinara sauce, bay leaf, parsley, cilantro, garlic, soy sauce, and apple cider vinegar. Bring to a boil, reduce the heat to a simmer, and let cook, covered, for 10 minutes. Then pour the heated sauce over the meatballs and cover with foil or an oven-safe lid, and transfer to the oven to bake for 25 minutes. Uncover and check one meatball for doneness. The sauce should be bubbling, the meatballs tender and fragrant. Serve with a side of sautéed vegetables and garnish with a sprinkling of minced cilantro and parsley.

COOK'S NOTES

MEATBALLS:

1 pound ground turkey

2 tablespoons fresh flat-leaf parsley, minced, plus more for garnish

2 tablespoons fresh cilantro, minced, plus more for garnish

1 teaspoon garlic, minced

1 tablespoon soy sauce

1 teaspoon apple cider vinegar

1 teaspoon dried Italian seasoning

½ teaspoon sea salt or Sea Veg

1 tablespoon olive oil

SAUCE:

1 (15-ounce) bottle of jarred organic marinara sauce

1 dried bay leaf

2 tablespoons fresh parsley, minced

2 teaspoons fresh cilantro, minced

2 teaspoons garlic, minced

1 teaspoon soy sauce

1 teaspoon apple cider vinegar

Game-Day Buffalo Chicken Wings

SERVES 4 A healthy diet doesn't seem all that appealing when you're sitting in front of the television and cheering for your favorite team. However, this recipe will change your mind. Brown rice flour makes this a bit of a healthier option than the breading used for normal wings, without sacrificing your desire for scrumptious finger-lickin' Buffalo wings.

1½ pounds chicken wings (whatever style you desire)

¼ cup white distilled vinegar

2 cups cold water

2 tablespoons plus 1 teaspoon olive oil, divided

1 teaspoon ground cumin

1 teaspoon garlic powder

1 teaspoon poultry seasoning

½ teaspoon sea salt or Sea Veg

¼ cup brown rice flour

½ cup wing sauce of your choice

COOK'S NOTES

1. Rinse chicken wings in cold water and then place them in a bowl. Pour the white distilled vinegar over the chicken, add the cold water to cover the chicken, and let sit in vinegar water for 10 to 15 minutes. Then pour out the vinegar water, wash the wings off in cold water, and pat them dry with a few paper towels.

2. In a freezer-safe bag, add the wings, along with 1 teaspoon olive oil, ground cumin, garlic powder, poultry seasoning, and sea salt or Sea Veg. Close the bag and shake it up until the wings are evenly coated. Add the brown rice flour and give it one last shake.

3. Line a baking sheet with parchment paper; set aside. Preheat oven to 275 degrees F. In a large sauté pan set over medium-high heat, pour in the remaining 2 tablespoons of olive oil. When the oil is hot and shimmering, add the wings, searing them on each side for about 1 to 2 minutes. Transfer the seared chicken wings to a clean medium-size bowl and toss quickly with half the wing sauce (¼ cup).

4. Place the wings on the parchment-lined baking sheet and transfer to the oven to bake for 45 minutes, until thoroughly cooked and tender. After the 45-minute mark, take the wings out of the oven, turn the oven up to 400 degrees F, add ¼ cup more of the wing sauce, and toss wings on the baking sheet. Bake for an additional 10 minutes. These can be served with your favorite herb dipping sauce and sliced celery and carrots.

INTUITIVE MOMENTS

These wings are a hit in my house, especially among friends and family. My husband and kids love Buffalo wings, but I don't like all the unhealthy ingredients typically found in everyone's favorite game-day snack. So I tested and tried different, healthier ingredients until I found the perfect mix. The brown rice flour makes a big difference. The exclusion of butter—a standard part of most recipes—also makes a big difference. But the fact that these wings aren't fried removes all the guilt. My husband and kids were the real test. If my husband ate one wing, and then had another, I truly had the green light. My son saw his dad eating and loving them, and figured he was not going to miss out either! These wings spice up any game or gathering—without all the heavy, greasy standard ingredients.

COOK'S NOTES

Chicken in the Garden, LA's Favorite

SERVES 4 Get your camera ready for this chicken's close-up. The before and after moments of this beauty are so pretty. I like using fresh herbs and allowing it to slow cook. It's perfect for a Sunday or holiday dinner.

1. Rinse the chicken in cold water and then put it in a bowl. Add the white distilled vinegar, cover the chicken with cold water, and let it sit for 30 minutes. Then pour out the vinegar water and wash the chicken thoroughly under cold running water, patting it dry with a few paper towels.

2. Preheat oven to 250 degrees F. Remove the chicken from the bowl and transfer it to a large pot (with an oven-safe lid) or Dutch oven. Rub the chicken with olive oil and sprinkle with sea salt or Sea Veg. Sprinkle salt in the cavity of the chicken and stuff the cavity with a few of the lemon pieces, some garlic cloves, and some sprigs of rosemary and thyme, as well as some sage leaves. Place the remaining quarters of lemon around the chicken, along with the remaining garlic cloves and herbs. The chicken should be completely covered with herbs. Cover the pot with a lid and transfer to the oven to roast for 4 hours, basting it with its own juices every 30 minutes or so.

3. After 4 hours, uncover the pot, remove the herbs that are covering the top of the chicken (so the herbs do not burn while broiling), and reserve for later. Turn the broiler on high for 5 to 10 minutes or until the chicken is golden brown. Keep a close eye on it while it's broiling. Set a timer as a reminder if needed so the chicken does not get scorched and you do not burn down the house! Serve the chicken alongside the reserved herbs.

1 (4-pound) chicken

½ cup white distilled vinegar

2 tablespoons olive oil

1½ teaspoon sea salt or Sea Veg

2 lemons, quartered

6 garlic cloves, peeled

1 small bunch fresh rosemary

1 small bunch fresh thyme sprigs

1 small bunch fresh sage leaves

INTUITIVE MOMENTS

Add some color to your cooking. That's how I discovered this chicken recipe, which has become a regular in our home. Covered with herbs and slow cooked until the meat simply falls off the bone, this recipe was seemingly the perfect mistake. I knew I wanted to add fresh herbs to make my typical baked chicken more colorful and flavorful. But I'll admit that I didn't have a plan the first time I made this. I just added a bunch of fresh herbs that I had left over in the refrigerator. And then I decided to slow cook the dish, simply because I knew we wouldn't be able to eat for many hours. Well, I created something that was beyond my imagination. And my husband absolutely loves it. Basically, I can get away with anything when I make this dish! This is a great (if not the greatest) Sunday chicken in our home.

Turkey Bacon–Wrapped Asparagus

SERVES 3 The salty flavor of the turkey bacon, combined with the distinct flavor of asparagus, will have everyone at the table asking for more.

½ pound asparagus
(about 15 spears)

8 ounces turkey bacon
(at least 3 slices)

1 teaspoon olive oil

Pinch of sea salt
or Sea Veg

Minced flat-leaf
Italian parsley or
cilantro, for garnish

1. Preheat oven to 400 degrees F. Line a baking sheet with parchment paper. Divide the asparagus into 3 bundles (5 asparagus spears each). Gather the first bundle of asparagus, wrap it with a slice of turkey bacon, and place it onto the baking sheet. Repeat with the remaining 2 bundles of asparagus and turkey bacon.

2. Drizzle the asparagus with a tiny bit of olive oil, and top the tips with a pinch of sea salt or Sea Veg.

3. Transfer to the oven to cook for 15 to 17 minutes, until the asparagus is bright green in color and the turkey bacon is crispy on its edges. Garnish with minced Italian parsley or cilantro.

COOK'S NOTES

Family Turkey Meatloaf

SERVES 4 TO 6 Nothing says home cooking like meatloaf. My kids happily eat this and even go for seconds. I like using quinoa to make the meatloaf more creative and filling. I suggest some veggies as a side dish, like the Cauliflower Rice Salad with Green Beans and Chickpeas (page 40) or the Avocado Carrot Salad (page 67).

1 teaspoon olive oil

3 pounds ground turkey

1 cup of cooked quinoa

¼ cup fresh flat-leaf parsley, minced

1 tablespoon fresh cilantro, minced

3 tablespoons soy sauce

1 tablespoon apple cider vinegar

1 tablespoon garlic powder

1 tablespoon dried Italian seasoning

1½ teaspoons sea salt or Sea Veg

¼ cup ketchup

1. Preheat oven to 350 degrees F. Use a paper towel dipped in a teaspoon of olive oil to grease an 8 × 5-inch loaf pan and set aside.

2. In a large bowl, combine the ground turkey, quinoa, parsley, cilantro, soy sauce, apple cider vinegar, garlic powder, dried Italian seasoning, and sea salt or Sea Veg. Don't be shy to get in there with your hands and really mix away. Transfer the turkey mixture to the loaf pan and shape the top so it has a slight mound to resemble a loaf of bread. Spread the ketchup atop the turkey mixture and transfer to the oven. Bake for 45 minutes to 1 hour, until the meat loaf is very firm to the touch and it is cooked throughout.

COOK'S NOTES

INTUITIVE MOMENTS

My mother made meatloaf on Sundays for me and my sisters when I lived at home. It would fill the house with the smell of comfort. And it seemed to create a sense of family togetherness because it's one of those meals where you don't serve people individual portions. You present the meatloaf to the table and let everyone grab for themselves. However, the older I get, the more I realize that my mom was probably making turkey meatloaf for other reasons as well. As a single mom who worked different shifts, she didn't always have time to cook during the week or weekend. And meatloaf leftovers can stretch through the week and become fantastic lunches and snacks.

Years ago, I had leftover quinoa and was curious what would happen if I added it to the ground turkey meat. It was an immediate hit because it adds great texture, nutrition, and heartiness.

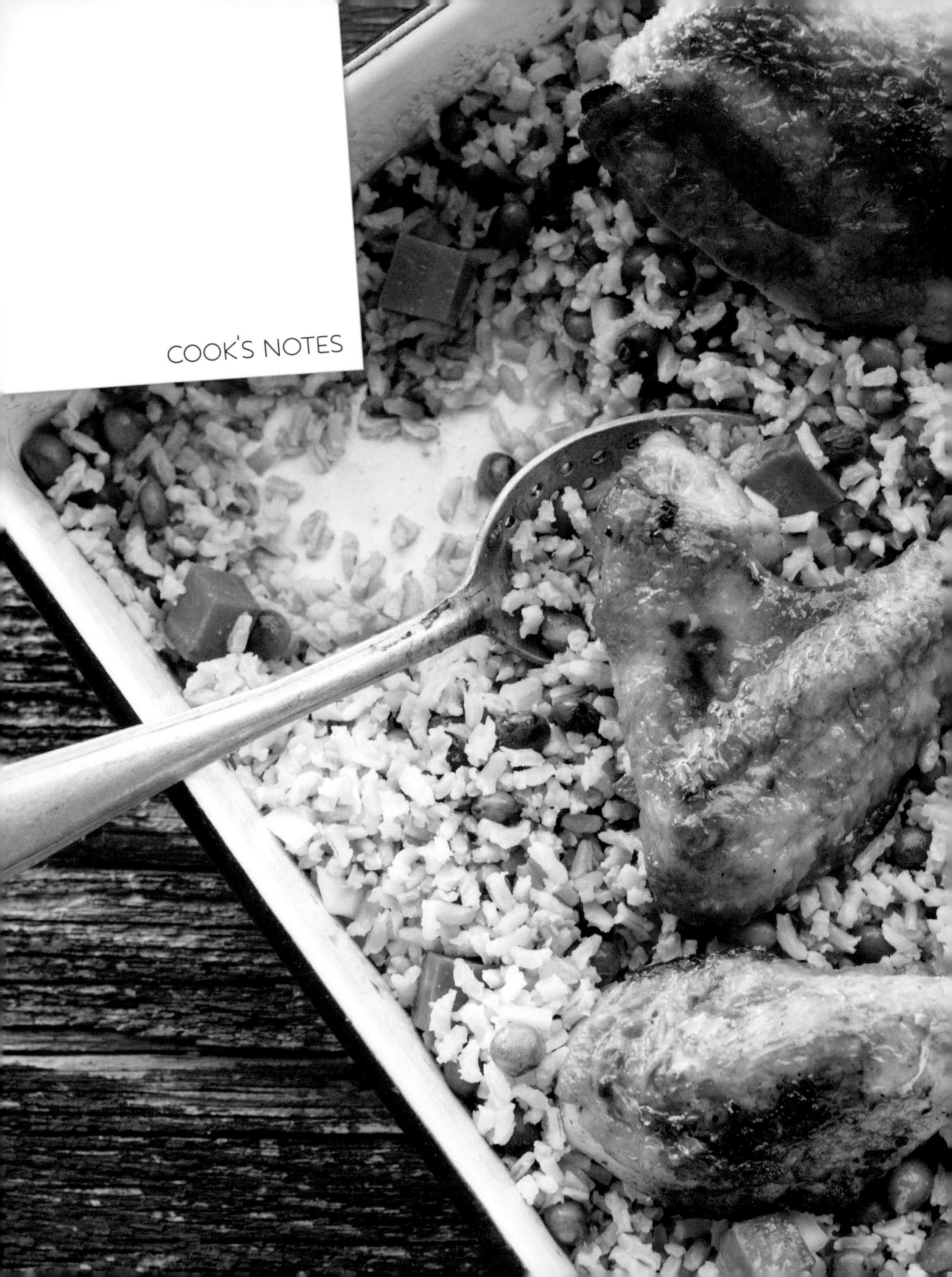

COOK'S NOTES

Mom's Bliss Pelau Chicken, My Way

SERVES 4 TO 6 Ready to taste a faraway land? Flavors from around the world can truly spice up your life. This dish will make you feel like you're sitting on an exotic Caribbean island. This is a wholesome hit with my family and I'm sure it will be with yours! Plus, the leftovers are simply amazing the next day.

1. Rinse the chicken in cold water and then cut up the chicken into parts. Put the chicken in a bowl, add the white vinegar, cover the chicken with cold water, and let soak for 15 minutes. Then pour off the vinegar water, rinse in cold water, and pat dry. Sprinkle the chicken with the sea salt or Sea Veg on both sides.

2. In a large pot or Dutch oven set over medium heat, add the maple syrup, caramelizing the syrup for about 2 minutes, until fragrant. Next, pour in the olive oil; when the oil is hot, add the chicken, skin-side down, cooking on each side for about 5 minutes. Depending on how big your pot is, you may need to do this in batches.

3. If you browned the chicken in batches, add all of the chicken back to the pot. Add 1 cup of water, the chicken stock, carrots, onion, and thyme. Bring the mixture to a simmer and then immediately turn the heat down to medium low, cooking for about 15 minutes, until the liquid has reduced by almost half.

4. Next, pour in the remaining 2 cups of water, brown rice, and cooked black-eyed peas or pigeon peas. Give the mixture a stir, making sure the rice is covered in the liquid. Cook for about 35 minutes, until the rice is tender. Divide between plates and garnish with a few cilantro leaves.

1 (3-pound) chicken

½ cup white distilled vinegar

2 teaspoons sea salt or Sea Veg

1 tablespoon maple syrup

2 tablespoons olive oil

3 cups water, divided

1 cup chicken stock, store-bought or homemade

½ cup diced carrots (from 1 carrot)

¼ cup finely minced yellow onion (from about ¼ onion)

1 teaspoon fresh thyme leaves (from 2 sprigs)

2 cups brown long-grain rice

¾ cup cooked black-eyed peas (recipe on page 61) or pigeon peas

Handful of cilantro leaves, for garnish

INTUITIVE MOMENTS

Bliss is not just a great description of what this recipe does for your senses; it's the name of my mother's best friend, who introduced her to the recipe. My mother's dearest friend was from Trinidad and had introduced my mom to many rich island flavors. As kids, we loved this dish so much. We ate it often. Today, my kids love it just as much. Of course, my mother still comes over to the house and makes it for the kids. This recipe doesn't use the traditional coconut. My mom also used pigeon peas, a legume popular throughout tropical areas, but you can replace those with black-eyed peas. You can add some extra hot sauce on top to kick up the spice and give it some more island richness.

Lamb and Other Meats

Did You Know?

Grass-fed means the animal is raised on a fresh forage-based diet in its own natural environment.

Mom's Staple Kielbasa with Sauerkraut

SERVES 4 For those who don't eat meat, replace kielbasa with tempeh. Both are complemented by the flavorful warm sauerkraut, which, if you didn't know, has numerous health benefits, like giving you good bacteria in your stomach. It's delicious, easy to prepare, and extremely economical.

1. In a medium sauté pan set over medium heat, pour in the olive oil. When hot, add the kielbasa or tempeh. Cook on the first side until lightly browned, about 3 minutes. Flip over and cook on the opposite side for an additional 3 minutes. Top with the sauerkraut and cook for an additional minute or so, until the kraut is warmed. Serve immediately with a side of mustard and garnish with parsley.

1 tablespoon olive oil

14 ounces turkey kielbasa, sliced in half lengthwise, or 14 ounces of tempeh, sliced

1½ cups sauerkraut

Mustard, for serving

Handful of flat-leaf Italian parsley, for garnish

COOK'S NOTES

INTUITIVE MOMENTS

This classic German meal is not only always a hit, but literally takes five minutes to prepare for yourself or your family. My mother used to make this dish for us all the time, and I honestly don't know where she got the recipe. But I do think back about the dish and can only assume that it meant one of two things. One, she was either waiting on payday (because the meal is inexpensive and easy to have on hand), or, two, she didn't feel like cooking. Whatever the reason, we always appreciated it, because it was prepared for us, and it was always pretty good. I cannot believe I still make this dish all these years later. Don't let the stigma fool you, though. There's plenty of protein in the kielbasa and nutrition in the sauerkraut to satisfy your appetite.

Rosemary Lamb Chops

SERVES 4 Rosemary and lamb both have very specific and recognizable flavors. Together, they become amazing. I personally prefer using fresh rosemary with this recipe because the smell is absolutely divine. Try this even if you're not typically a fan of lamb. It makes my friends and children say "Yummmm!"

---

1 pound of ¾-inch-thick lamb chops, rinsed and patted dry

¼ cup balsamic vinegar

1 tablespoon apple cider vinegar

Sea salt or Sea Veg

2 tablespoons olive oil, divided

2 garlic cloves, minced

3 sprigs fresh rosemary

4 to 8 lettuce leaves, for serving

4 cooked lemon halves, for serving

1. In a medium bowl, combine the lamb chops, balsamic vinegar, apple cider vinegar, and a few pinches of sea salt or Sea Veg. Give it a mix and allow to marinate in the fridge for 30 minutes.

2. Preheat oven to 350 degrees F. In a large sauté pan set over medium-high heat, add one tablespoon olive oil. When the oil is hot, add the garlic and sprigs of rosemary. Top the garlic and rosemary with the lamb chops and cook on each side for 2 to 3 minutes, until lightly browned. Transfer the sauté pan to the oven to bake for 30 minutes, until medium well.

3. Place another sauté pan over medium heat and pour in the remaining tablespoon of olive oil. Once the oil is hot, add the lamb chops and sear on both sides for an additional 30 seconds. This makes them extra crispy! Serve on a bed of 2 lettuce leaves with a lemon half.

COOK'S NOTES

INTUITIVE MOMENTS

Need a twist on your typical dinner? Try lamb chops. I kept seeing lamb on the menu at so many restaurants that it made me wonder if it's something the family would enjoy at home. Of course, the first time I tried making lamb chops, it was just an experiment. But it didn't take me long to figure out the right combination of rosemary and garlic to make my family coo over this dish. My kids love them. The chops add some variety into daily life; they can also be served at a dinner party when guests might be expecting a surprise.

As soon as I tried cooking lamb, I knew it would be a challenge to get the gamey smell out of the house. I quickly discovered that by adding apple cider vinegar to the recipe, the odor is greatly diminished . . . and the flavor is fantastic!

Savory Lamb Burgers

SERVES 4 Burgers are a staple in most households. They're usually the meal of choice at outdoor gatherings and the meal of choice when people are on the go. But, I think we can do better—healthier, tastier, and more unique. Plus, I've always thought that if kids like a recipe (which mine do), you know you've created a hit! Serve these burgers without first mentioning that they're made from lamb. You'll be shocked by the smiling faces around your table!

---

1. In a large bowl, combine the ground lamb, parsley, cilantro, soy sauce, apple cider vinegar, garlic powder, and sea salt or Sea Veg. Scoop out ¼ cup mixture at a time and form 4 patties.

2. In a medium sauté pan set over medium heat, add the olive oil. When the oil is hot, add the patties and cook on each side for 3 to 5 minutes, until firm to the touch. Place the lamb burgers in between two buns or wrap them in lettuce.

1 pound ground lamb

1 tablespoon flat-leaf Italian parsley, minced

1 tablespoon fresh cilantro, minced

1 teaspoon soy sauce

1 teaspoon apple cider vinegar

½ teaspoon garlic powder

¼ teaspoon sea salt or Sea Veg

1 tablespoon olive oil

Gluten-free hamburger buns or lettuce, for serving

COOK'S NOTES

Did You Know?

Macronutrients are the primary nutrients in foods such as protein and carbohydrates.

Fish

Ginger Salmon

SERVES 4 Ginger is one of my favorite spices because it has so many healing health benefits and adds a ton of flavor. I like to use it on salmon—my loved ones are not eating something that tastes "fishy" while also receiving important nutrients. Salmon is loaded with omega-3 oils, which have been known to reduce inflammation and to be great for your heart and brain.

1 pound salmon,
cut into 4 fillets

2-inch knob fresh
ginger, grated

¼ teaspoon sea
salt or Sea Veg

¼ cup low-sodium soy
sauce or shoyu soy sauce

2 tablespoons olive oil

Cooked leeks, for serving

Handful of micro
greens, for garnish

1. Rinse salmon in cold water and then place in a medium bowl; rub the grated ginger all over the salmon fillets. Sprinkle with sea salt or Sea Veg. Pour in the soy sauce, cover the bowl with plastic wrap, and transfer to the fridge to marinate for 3 hours.

2. Pour the olive oil into a large sauté pan set over medium-high heat. When the oil is hot and glistens, add the salmon, skin side down, and cook for 4 to 6 minutes. Divide the fillets of salmon between plates and serve immediately. Serve with cooked leeks and garnish with a bit of micro greens.

NOTE: *If you don't have the 3 hours to marinate the salmon, no biggie! I skip the marinating time and go straight to cooking it in the pan.*

COOK'S NOTES

INTUITIVE MOMENTS

Eating healthy can be fun. I had been cooking salmon for years simply because it's loaded with essential oils that are so good for us. The question was: How do I make salmon even more delicious? How do I make it taste like it's more of a delicacy? This recipe gives this healthy fish a twist you and your family will appreciate—with a zing from the ginger that will surely get people asking for more. Plus, leftovers go great on top of salad the next day for lunch!

Miso Cod en Papillote

SERVES 4 Cod—a cold water white fish—offers tons of vitamins and nutrients such as high amounts of B12. As a result, this recipe is a frequent visitor in our home—it's super healthy, delicious, and surprisingly easy to prepare. Bake it. Never fry it. Frying basically eliminates all the benefits and adds numerous negatives! You'll love this.

---

1. Preheat oven to 350 degrees F.

2. To assemble, add a few slices of lemon to the center of a sheet of parchment and then top with one cod fillet. Next, add a few pieces of carrots and asparagus. Top with a squeeze of lemon juice, and lastly, drizzle with oil and top with a pinch of sea salt or Sea Veg. Bring the top seams of the parchment together and fold over a few times, like you would a brown paper bag. Fold in the sides a few times, making sure no air can escape. Repeat with the remaining fillets of cod and veggies. Transfer them to a baking sheet and place in the oven for about 15 minutes.

3. While the cod is cooking, make the miso topping. In a small pot, add the water and bring to a boil. Turn the heat off and cool the water so it's just warm to the touch. (Make sure the water is warm, not hot, as hot water kills all of miso's good bacteria and nutrients.) Add the miso to the pot and whisk together until smooth. The mixture should be cloudy and on the thinner side. Remove the baking sheet from the oven and carefully undo the seams on the parchment bundles to allow the hot air to escape. Spoon about a tablespoon of the miso mixture over each piece of cod. Transfer each piece of fish, parchment and all, to individual plates and garnish with micro greens. Serve immediately.

1 lemon, sliced into rounds

1 pound cod, cut into 4 fillets, washed in cold water and patted dry

1 carrot, thinly sliced

½ bunch of asparagus, trimmed and sliced on the diagonal

A bit of squeezed lemon juice

2 teaspoons olive oil

Sea salt or Sea Veg

½ cup water

1 tablespoon plain white miso

Micro greens, for garnish

COOK'S NOTES

Salmon "Sushi" Rolls

SERVES 2: 12 CUT PIECES OF SUSHI ROLL That's right! You can make sushi at home. It is not from the famous Japanese restaurant Nobu, but it is famous from my house to yours. Simple and easy is what impressed me when I first played around with making this. Stop thinking that you need to take a sushi class to make your own at home.

¾ cup brown rice

1 strip kombu

1½ cups water

Sea salt or Sea Veg (skip salt if using umeboshi paste)

1 tablespoon olive oil

1 (4-ounce) fillet of salmon

2 sheets toasted nori

2 teaspoons umeboshi paste, divided (optional)

1. In a medium saucepan set over medium heat, add the brown rice, kombu, water, and sea salt or Sea Veg, if using. Bring the water to a simmer and immediately reduce the heat to medium low. Cover and cook for about 20 minutes, until the water has evaporated and the rice is cooked throughout. Fluff the rice and set aside.

2. In a medium sauté pan set over medium-high heat, pour in the olive oil. If using umeboshi paste, skip salting the salmon. If not, then be sure to sprinkle the salmon with a few pinches of sea salt or Sea Veg. When the oil is hot, add the salmon, skin side down, and cook, covered, for about 4 to 6 minutes. Transfer the salmon to a plate and flake using two forks. Allow to cool completely.

3. Set out the sheets of nori on a cutting board. Spread a thin layer of umeboshi paste on each, about 1 teaspoon per sheet. Divide the rice among the nori and spread it on the first half of the sheet closest to you. Top with half of the flaked salmon. Rub the top seam with a bit of water and roll the sushi tightly. Cut the sushi into ¾-inch pieces and serve.

NOTE: *You can also use short-grain "sushi" brown rice, which is fantastic, but keep in mind that the cook time will be a bit longer, around 45 minutes.*

COOK'S NOTES

Gluten-Free Salmon Pea Pasta

SERVES 6 How do you cook something easy and tasty? Life gets hectic sometimes and we can all find ourselves eating on autopilot. This recipe is a game changer for anyone who wants full flavor without hours of work or guilt. The zest of the lemon makes this hearty pasta dish divine.

1. Pour a tablespoon of olive oil into a medium sauté pan set over medium-high heat Sprinkle the piece of salmon with a few pinches of sea salt or Sea Veg. When the oil is hot, add the salmon, skin side down, and cook, covered, for about 4 to 6 minutes. Transfer the salmon to a plate and flake using two forks. Allow to cool completely.

2. Bring a large pot of water to a boil. Add the pasta and cook until tender, al dente, or according to the package's instructions. Drain the pasta and add back to the pot.

3. Bring a small saucepan filled with water to a boil. Add the peas and cook for about 1 minute. Drain the peas and add them to the pot with the pasta. Add two tablespoons of olive oil, a pinch of sea salt or Sea Veg, and lemon zest, and toss. Lastly, mix in the flaked salmon and a few pinches of sea salt or Sea Veg to taste. Divide among the bowls.

3 tablespoons olive oil, divided

½ pound salmon fillet

Sea salt or Sea Veg

1 pound gluten-free fusilli pasta

2 cups frozen peas

Zest from ½ lemon

Shut Up and Listen

I love to eat. I really enjoy food that tastes good. I eat to fuel myself and to feel vibrant and naturally energized. I don't want to feel heavy, sleepy, sluggish, or either struggling to start my day or straining to get through the end of my day. Food can make you feel the way you want—or the way you don't want. It's your choice. You have the power to make that final decision. So make it: Decide how you want to feel and eat appropriately.

COOK'S NOTES

Dressings
and Sauces

Avocado Dressing

YIELD: ½ CUP Do you ever wonder how you can add your favorite foods to more dishes? When I love something, like avocados, I like to incorporate that flavor in other recipes. Plus, the healthy fat offered by avocados turns any great salad into a nutritional powerhouse.

2 tablespoons water

2 teaspoons apple cider vinegar

1 avocado, pitted and peeled

1 tablespoon vegan mayonnaise

1 teaspoon nutritional yeast

Sea salt or Sea Veg, to taste

1. Combine the water, apple cider vinegar, avocado, vegan mayonnaise, nutritional yeast, and pinch of sea salt or Sea Veg in a blender. Pulse until smooth, about 1 minute. Adjust the salt according to taste.

COOK'S NOTES

Lemon Dressing

YIELD: ⅔ CUP I've told you that food is medicine. This dressing is medicine for both the body and soul! The vitamin C in lemons makes this a constant fixture in our medicine cabinet (refrigerator) to boost the immune system. And the flavor adds freshness to even the most bland foods.

Juice from 2 lemons
(about 3 tablespoons)

⅓ cup olive oil

Pinch of sea salt
or Sea Veg

1. In a small bowl, whisk together the lemon juice, olive oil, and a pinch of sea salt or Sea Veg.

Did You Know?

First thing in the morning, adding a bit of fresh-squeezed lemon to plain room temperature water is known to cleanse the liver and get your digestive system moving.

COOK'S NOTES

Herbed Salad Dressing

YIELD: ⅓ CUP Nature is bursting with the most interesting flavors. I don't care if you just throw lettuce in a bowl; the fresh herbs in this dressing (added to anything, really) can make any recipe taste great. Plus, some of the possible health benefits this dressing offers turn any salad into a supersalad!

¼ cup olive oil

1. In a small bowl or mason jar, add the olive oil, basil, sage, rosemary leaves, oregano, and sea salt or Sea Veg. Cover with plastic wrap or lid and allow to marinate for at least 4 hours, or up to 24 hours. Toss the dressing in a salad with a squeeze of half a lemon.

4 fresh basil leaves

2 fresh sage leaves

Leaves from 2 sprigs of fresh rosemary

¼ teaspoon dried oregano

Pinch of sea salt or Sea Veg

Juice from ½ lemon, optional

COOK'S NOTES

Teriyaki Sauce

YIELD: ⅔ CUP You may already have a bottle of teriyaki sauce in your refrigerator. And you might be thinking, "Why make it?" But, honestly, have you ever looked at some of the sauces in your kitchen and wondered, "When did I buy that? How old is it? How long did it sit on the shelf at the store before I bought it?" Friends, homemade is always better. It tastes better. It's comforting to know exactly what the ingredients are. And you know it's fresh. I love to brush this teriyaki sauce on baked chicken or baked tofu.

½ cup soy sauce

1 tablespoon agave nectar

½-inch knob
ginger, grated

1 scallion, thinly sliced

1. In a medium bowl, whisk together the soy sauce, agave, ginger, and scallion.

Did You Know?

Some condiments such as ketchup and soy sauce can contain gluten.

COOK'S NOTES

Maple Cider Vinaigrette

YIELD: A SCANT ½ CUP Sometimes the strangest ideas you have in the kitchen become the most prized. Maple syrup isn't just for pancakes, people! The combination of the sweetness from the syrup mixed with vinegar creates a neutralizing tanginess that makes this dressing so good on any salad.

⅓ cup apple cider vinegar

1 tablespoon maple syrup

Pinch of sea salt or Sea Veg

1. In a small bowl, whisk together the apple cider vinegar, maple syrup, and sea salt or Sea Veg.

COOK'S NOTES

INTUITIVE MOMENTS

Salad dressing doesn't have to come in a bottle. Yep, it was a surprise to me, too! I honestly didn't realize you could make salad dressing from scratch. And it took me a long time to learn that many of the bottled dressings you buy are loaded with a ton of ingredients to keep it where it can live in that bottle. I surely didn't want my loved ones ingesting all those additives, especially at home, where there are choices. So I started playing around with ingredients I love—maple syrup and vinaigrette. Give this recipe a try—I think you'll be shocked and amazed by the flavor a fresh dressing can add to your favorite salad. I honestly don't remember the last time I bought bottled salad dressing—I know what I make is fresh; I know what's in it; I know it's delicious.

Plum Sauce

YIELD: ⅔ CUP Plums aren't just legendary from children's stories! They can be used for so many recipes due to their unique flavor. This mixture makes a great dipping sauce to have with the veggie rolls on page 68.

½ pound (about 2) black plums, pitted and chopped

¼ cup organic apple juice

Freshly squeezed lemon juice, optional

1. In a small saucepan set over medium heat, pour in the chopped black plums and apple juice. Bring the mixture to a boil and cook for 10 to 15 minutes. Next, pour the plum mixture into a blender and pulse until smooth.

2. If you like, you can run the mixture through a strainer. If the plum sauce is too thick, add a bit more apple juice until you've reached your desired consistency. To add a bit more tartness, mix in the juice from a lemon.

> **Did You Know?**
>
> *"Organic" means, basically, that a food has not been sprayed with pesticides or treated with growth hormones.*

COOK'S NOTES

Soups

Broth

YIELD: APPROXIMATELY 3½ QUARTS Grocery stores offer an abundance of packaged soup. When I make any homemade soup for myself and my loved ones, I know they are getting ingredients that are fresh and full of flavor, as well as nutrients and vitamins.

6 quarts of water

3 ribs of celery, chopped

3 carrots, chopped

3 garlic cloves, peeled

1 small handful curly or Italian parsley

1 yellow onion, peeled and quartered

¼ cup dried shitake mushrooms, rinsed

1 strip kombu

½ teaspoon ground turmeric

1. In a large pot set over high heat, pour in the water. Add the celery, carrots, garlic, parsley, onion, shitake mushrooms, kombu, and turmeric. Give it a thorough mix, cover the pot, and bring the broth to a boil; immediately turn the heat to low and allow the broth to simmer, about 2 hours.

2. Run the broth through a strainer, discarding the vegetables and any bits. Divide the broth among quart containers and cover. Use immediately or transfer to the freezer for later use. To thaw, transfer to the fridge for 2 to 3 hours, or allow to stand on the kitchen counter for 1 to 2 hours.

COOK'S NOTES

INTUITIVE MOMENTS

I truly never imaged that I could make my own broth, or that I could make it taste so delicious. I had to give it a try because I didn't want to buy broth in a can or box; I wanted to see the vegetables used to create the broth. But I had no idea of where to even start. So, I went home, looked at the vegetables I had in the refrigerator, threw them in a pot with water, and brought the pot to a boil. I had also seen chefs throw out boiled vegetables (because the nutrients are dissipated after long cooking times) so I figured I would strain the boiled vegetables out of mine as well. It was so easy. And it was quite a surprise that I could actually do it myself.

Honed after many, many trials and errors (like too much of one vegetable and not enough of another), this recipe provides outstanding flavor and nutrition. It's easy to make, easy to tweak to your liking (for instance, if you want more mushroom flavor, add more mushrooms), and convenient to make more than you need so you can freeze it for future recipes.

Black Bean Soup

SERVES 4 TO 6 Black beans, in anything, are a favorite of mine. But beans often get a bad rap for making our stomachs flutter. It took some time, but I learned how to prepare this soup so that my system never gets irritated. My cravings get fulfilled. My hunger gets curbed. And, we all get the nutritional benefits of the best—in my opinion—little bean on earth. This recipe is great when topped with the tofu cream.

1. In a blender, add the liquid (water or cooking liquid from beans or vegetable stock), apple cider vinegar, beans, cilantro leaves, and sea salt or Sea Veg. Pulse until very smooth. The soup's texture should be on the thinner side. Pour 1 teaspoon olive oil in a medium pot and sauté the onion and garlic for 2 to 3 minutes. Pour the blended bean mixture over the onions and garlic and stir; cook and stir for 5 minutes or until heated through.

2. Meanwhile, in a small bowl, whisk together the tofu cream cheese and rice milk until smooth. Divide the soup between the bowls, and add a drizzle of the tofu cream to each bowl.

SOUP:

1 cup water or cooking liquid from beans, or vegetable stock

1 teaspoon apple cider vinegar

2½ cups Yum-Yum Black Beans (recipe on page 55)

⅓ cup cilantro leaves

½ teaspoon sea salt or Sea Veg

1 teaspoon olive oil

½ yellow onion, chopped

2 garlic cloves, minced

TOFU CREAM:

¼ cup soy cream cheese

2 teaspoons rice milk

COOK'S NOTES

INTUITIVE MOMENTS

This fiber-rich soup recipe is irresistible—and, I confess, it was an absolute mistake the first time I made it. Imagine, for a second, those times when you're in the kitchen. Maybe you're preparing two or three dishes at the same time. Maybe you're distracted by your kids, or caught up in your favorite song (dancing in the kitchen is not out of the question in my house). Well, that was me. I overcooked my black beans. They were too soft to serve so I decided to put them in the blender and add some spices, and, the next thing I knew, I had created a hearty, savory soup that has become a beloved staple in my home.

Green Soup

SERVES 6 We never get enough greens. Even the healthiest eaters need more, as greens are so vital to our well-being and fighting diseases. Kale is seriously the new black of the food world. This leafy green vegetable creates a soup that you won't be able to get enough of—no matter how much you make! I love adding the crispy chips for an extra *oomph*, and my daughter and her friends love snacking on these chips.

1. To make the kale chips, preheat oven to 300 degrees F. On a parchment-lined baking sheet, spread out the kale leaves and drizzle with olive oil and sea salt or Sea Veg. Toss until they're evenly coated. Transfer to the oven and bake until crispy, about 15 to 20 minutes. Remove from oven and set aside to cool.

2. To make the soup, pour the olive oil in a medium pot set over medium heat. When the oil is hot, add the leek and cook until softened, about 3 minutes. Next, add the broccoli florets and vegetable broth. Bring the mixture to a simmer and cook for 7 minutes, until the broccoli is bright green. Mix in the kale leaves, cover, and cook for an additional 7 minutes, until the broccoli is tender and the kale leaves are wilted.

3. Depending on the size of your blender, you may need to do the next step in batches. Transfer the soup to the blender and pulse until smooth, about 30 seconds. Mix in the vinegar and sea salt or Sea Veg. Give it a taste and adjust the salt or the umeboshi vinegar to your liking. Divide the soup between bowls and top with a few kale chips.

KALE CHIPS (SEE PHOTO ON PAGE 131):

1 bunch kale, stems removed and discarded

2 teaspoons olive oil

Pinch of sea salt or Sea Veg

KALE SOUP:

1 tablespoon olive oil

1 leek, white and pale green parts, sliced vertically

1 pound of broccoli florets (from about 2 stalks of broccoli)

1 quart vegetable broth, homemade (recipe on page 116) or store-bought

1 bunch kale, stems removed and discarded

2 tablespoons umeboshi vinegar

¼ teaspoon sea salt or Sea Veg

COOK'S NOTES

Shredded "Soup-Kitchen" Chicken Soup

SERVES 6 Here's a soup beloved by all age groups, especially on a brisk day when people want to feel warm and cozy. Of course, many of us grew up believing that chicken soup had healing powers when we were ill—and I believe, if you make it right, it does.

2 quarts cool water

3 stalks celery, sliced

2 medium carrots, diced

1 small yellow onion, finely minced

1 garlic clove, minced

1 strip kombu

¼ cup roughly chopped flat-leaf Italian parsley, plus more for garnish

1 skinless and boneless chicken breast

1 tablespoon apple cider vinegar

½ teaspoon umeboshi vinegar

½ teaspoon sea salt or Sea Veg

Cilantro, for garnish

1. In a large pot set over medium-high heat, add the cool water, celery, carrots, onion, garlic, kombu, parsley, chicken, and apple cider vinegar. Bring the mixture to a simmer and then immediately reduce the heat to medium low. Cook the soup for 45 minutes, until chicken is thoroughly cooked.

2. Remove the chicken and cool until you're able to handle it with your bare hands. Using your hands, shred the chicken by pulling it into thin shreds and then return it to the pot, adding the umeboshi vinegar and sea salt or Sea Veg. Give the soup a taste and adjust the salt or umeboshi vinegar to your liking. Divide among bowls and serve. Garnish with a few flat-leaf Italian parsley and cilantro leaves.

COOK'S NOTES

INTUITIVE MOMENTS

Chicken soup may get more accolades than the medical industry for curing the common cold. Somehow it magically soothes, comforts, and warms like nothing else. And chicken soup is one of my kids' favorite menu items at a New York restaurant where we often eat. Of course, when my kids had the sniffles, I wanted them to experience the magic of chicken soup, but without going to a restaurant, and surely not from a can.

Again, I had no clue where to start. I knew there was chicken. I knew there was celery. I knew there were garlic and carrots. But, beyond that, I didn't know how to put it all together into something amazing and delicious.

When I first started making chicken soup, I knew I was onto something. But there was also something missing. I was making the broth from scratch. I was cutting the chicken and vegetables in chunks. I was adding the perfect amounts of ingredients and garlic. But it wasn't until my husband, kids, and I volunteered at a soup kitchen that I learned what I was missing—I needed to shred the chicken, not cut it.

There we were: It was Thanksgiving Day, on Skid Row, in Los Angeles, California. My husband was a judge on *The X Factor* at the time. In fact, that day, they were airing a live episode where he was judging. We knew how fortunate and blessed we were to all be together and to be able to travel, to be able to attend such a big, live event on that holiday. It was very important to me to make sure that my children didn't get sidetracked by the show, so I made it our plan to share and give back to others before we headed to the studio. I believe in giving back to others not just on Thanksgiving Day, but every day. It was the perfect setting, the perfect city, and we made the time that morning to share our blessings with others. It was important and magical to us. My husband was about to entertain the world. Why shouldn't we take our free time in the morning to help and do for others?

Ironically, the blessings kept flowing. We met fantastic folks. We were serving, sharing, and helping many people. And, I never imagined it, but I was about to learn something I didn't expect—how to improve my chicken soup.

When we were assigned duties in the soup kitchen, I was given the task of pulling the turkey from the bone to add to the stuffing and gravy. The meat shredded beautifully. It was so obvious and simple. The only thing my soup was missing was shredded chicken—not chunked or cubed chicken the way I used to make it. I am so grateful we did that and I was given that responsibility.

When you make this soup, dig into the chicken with your hands! Shredding the chicken gives the soup a beautiful hearty texture and look, and it makes every spoonful absolutely delectable!

Cauliflower Soup

SERVES 4 TO 6 Cauliflower is one of my all-time favorite cruciferous vegetables—it provides fantastic health benefits. This soup is surprisingly fresh, a delicious combination of sweet and salty, and it's super easy and full of vitamins.

1 pound cauliflower, cut into florets

2 cups plus 1 or 2 tablespoons heated vegetable broth, homemade (recipe on page 116) or store-bought

3 tablespoons umeboshi vinegar

1 teaspoon sea salt or Sea Veg

Black sesame seeds, toasted (optional)

1. Bring a large pot of water to a boil. Drop the florets of cauliflower into the water and cook 12 to 15 minutes, until very tender. Drain and then transfer to a blender.

2. If vegetable stock is homemade or store-bought, it needs to be heated in a pot on the stove for 2-3 minutes on medium heat. Then, transfer the stock, umeboshi vinegar, and Sea Veg or sea salt. Blend until very smooth, 30 seconds to a minute, adding a splash or two more of broth if needed. Divide between bowls and serve immediately. Garnish with toasted sesame seeds, if you'd like.

COOK'S NOTES

INTUITIVE MOMENTS

The flavor of cooked cauliflower is one that seems to soothe the soul and warm the heart. Every time I ate cauliflower soup, I wondered what was in it—what makes it so delicious? Years ago, I taught myself to make a simple soup, so I figured I'd just get into the kitchen and give the same fearless try to cauliflower soup. Satisfaction comes easy with this recipe. Just boil down the cauliflower, blend it, and combine it with your homemade vegetable broth. The flavor is to die for, and the aroma will get your neighbors knocking on the door.

Soothing Butternut Soup

SERVES 6 Some recipes seem to do more than just fuel us with energy or fill our bellies. I can't exactly explain, but you know what I'm talking about—that warm sensation that somehow seems to touch your soul. The soft, gentle texture and the deep, rich flavor of this soup makes even the pickiest eaters want more.

1. In a medium to large pot set over medium heat, add olive oil and onion, and let the onion soften for 2 to 3 minutes. Add butternut squash and sweet potato; cover with vegetable broth. Bring to a boil and then immediately turn the heat down to a simmer and cook, covered, for 15 to 20 minutes or until vegetables are tender.

2. Transfer soup to a blender; add maple syrup, apple cider vinegar, and sea salt or Sea Veg. Blend until very smooth. Depending on how large your blender is, you may need to do this in batches. Give the soup a taste and adjust the salt according to your liking. Divide between bowls and garnish with a spoonful of tofu cream, toasted pumpkin seeds, and/or cilantro leaves.

1 teaspoon olive oil

1 onion, diced

1 butternut squash (about 2½ pounds), peeled and cubed

1 sweet potato, peeled and cubed

4 cups homemade (recipe on page 116) or store-bought vegetable broth

2 tablespoons maple syrup

½ teaspoon apple cider vinegar

½ teaspoon sea salt or Sea Veg

¼ cup tofu cream (in recipe for Black Bean Soup on page 117)

¼ cup pumpkin seeds, toasted, and/or ¼ cup cilantro, for garnish

COOK'S NOTES

INTUITIVE MOMENTS

I remember, as a young child, being at school during nap time and smelling cooked squash from the cafeteria, which, at the time, seemed just nasty to me. I couldn't stand the smell. I remember telling myself that I'll never eat that stinky squash—ever. I couldn't even take my nap because of that smell!

As I got older, I remember seeing squash soup dishes on menus at restaurants. Of course, at first, I thought about those nasty-smelling nap times when I was young. But then I became curious as to how the restaurants could sell that soup. Maybe there was something I didn't know.

As always, I went into my kitchen and tried to make it for myself. The first time I tried it, it was horrible. It smelled just like nap time. It tasted worse. I didn't get it right the second or third time either. But then I thought to add the sweet potato. The sweetness and texture made all my previous attempts pale in comparison. I squashed my horrible memories of squash.

Pizza

With Love, Arianna and Addison's Pizza

YIELD: 1 PIZZA It may be a little more work than dialing your local pizza joint or ordering online, but at least with this quick and easy pizza recipe, you'll know exactly what you and your family are eating. Plus, using fresh herbs and adding nutrients makes what you might have considered a "guilty meal" turn into a beneficial addition to your diet.

Olive oil

1 pound store-bought pizza dough, cut in half*

¼ cup jarred organic pizza marinara sauce**

½ cup shredded fresh mozzarella or nondairy shredded cheese mix***

¼ cup freshly chopped basil, divided

COOK'S NOTES

1. Preheat oven to 450 degrees F.

2. In a 10-inch cast-iron skillet, pour in a teaspoon or two of olive oil. Use a paper towel to go around the entire skillet to coat it so the dough will not stick to the pan while baking.

3. Stretch out the half ball of pizza dough, pressing it until it completely covers the bottom of the skillet. Evenly spread the marinara sauce on the top of the pizza dough and sprinkle with the shredded cheese of choice and half of the basil. Transfer to the preheated oven to bake for 15 to 20 minutes, until the edges are golden brown. Then turn your oven's setting to broil for about 1 to 2 minutes so the cheese can melt and also turn golden brown in color. Use a spatula to get under the pizza and transfer to a cutting board. Garnish with the rest of the chopped basil leaves.

* The pizza dough I like to buy is from Whole Foods. It comes in a frozen ball that weighs 1 pound. For this recipe, be sure to cut the ball in half once it is completely thawed so that you use only a half pound of dough per pizza. You can thaw the dough out in the refrigerator or on the kitchen counter for 1 to 2 hours.

** I love spicing up a jar of organic pizza sauce by pouring it into a bowl and adding a few of my favorite fresh seasonings: ½ teaspoon soy sauce, pinch of salt to taste, ½ teaspoon fresh cilantro, and ½ teaspoon fresh basil. After this is all mixed up, it's ready for the pizzas!

*** Follow Your Heart is my favorite brand of meltable nondairy cheese.

INTUITIVE MOMENTS

Every Friday night is pizza night at our house. Of course, it's probably pizza night in many homes because people want to relax, have fun, and de-stress. We sometimes don't want to cook after a full week of work and all our other activities. But if you get a pizza delivered, you don't always know what's in it. And, quite honestly, my family prefers homemade pizza over delivery. Plus, if your family is anything like mine, dietary restrictions can make ordering in difficult—especially for the people taking the order.

At one point, Addison, my son, was not able to tolerate dairy so I use a grated nondairy cheese for him. Arianna, my daughter, had no problem with dairy on her pizza so I use mozzarella for her. Both kids get a delicious pizza. I know what I'm feeding them and everyone is happy. Usually I prefer the nondairy option for the whole family since it's healthier and I rarely keep dairy cheese in the house. These pizzas are so good that my sister will often call on Fridays and ask, "Are you guys making pizza?" She knows we're having fun eating something that is not going to spoil our Friday evening later.

Three-Cheese Veggie Pizza

SERVES 1 TO 2 Indulge and feel good because you made this pizza at home instead of ordering it from a place that doesn't care about your health. You'll be amazed by how tasty you can make eating healthy, especially when you experience the outstanding blend of melty, gooey cheeses in this recipe.

3 brussels sprouts

1 to 2 teaspoons olive oil

1 pound store-bought pizza dough, cut in half (see note on page 126)

¼ cup jarred pizza marinara sauce

¼ cup lightly packed kale leaves, torn

¼ cup fresh basil leaves

¼ cup sliced cremini mushrooms or shiitake mushrooms

¼ cup shredded white cheddar mozzarella or regular mozzarella cheese

¼ cup crumbled feta

¼ cup goat cheese

1. Preheat oven to 450 degrees F. Start by separating the leaves of the brussels sprouts, one by one. You should end up with about a cup of brussels sprouts leaves.

2. In a 10-inch cast iron skillet, pour in a teaspoon or two of olive oil. Use a paper towel to go around the entire skillet to coat it so the dough will not stick to the pan while baking.

3. Stretch out the ball of pizza dough, pressing it until it completely covers the bottom. Evenly spread the marinara sauce on the top of the pizza dough and add the kale leaves, brussels sprouts leaves, basil, and mushrooms. Sprinkle the cheddar, feta, and goat cheese all around. Transfer to the preheated oven to bake for 15 to 20 minutes, until the edges are golden brown. Then turn your oven's setting to broil to melt the mozzarella cheese and until the feta (mainly) and goat cheese get a little toasted in color, about 1 to 2 minutes. Use a spatula to get under the pizza and transfer to a cutting board to slice.

COOK'S NOTES

Pesto Avocado Pizza

SERVES 1 Add flavor and essential oils to your ordinary pizza. Yes, pizza and super-nutritious vegetables can go hand in hand if they are done right! The garlic and basil flavor pop on your taste buds and make this recipe stand out over pizzas that use more traditional tomato based sauces.

1. Preheat oven to 450 degrees F. In a food processor, add the kale leaves, olive oil, garlic, and sea salt or Sea Veg. Pulse until mostly smooth. Set aside.

2. In a 10-inch cast-iron skillet, pour in a teaspoon of olive oil. Use a paper towel to go around the entire skillet to coat it so the dough will not stick to the pan while baking.

3. Stretch out the half ball of pizza dough, pressing it until it mostly covers the bottom of the pan. Evenly spread the kale pesto on top of the pizza dough and sprinkle with the shredded cheese. Transfer to the preheated oven to bake for 15 to 20 minutes, until the edges are golden brown. Turn your oven's setting to broil for about 1 to 2 minutes so the cheese can melt and turn golden brown in color. Use a spatula to get under the pizza and transfer to a cutting board.

4. Meanwhile, in a small bowl, toss the arugula with the remaining 1 teaspoon of olive oil, lemon juice, and pinch of sea salt or Sea Veg. Top the pizza with the arugula and cubed avocado.

COOK'S NOTES

KALE PESTO:

1 cup lightly packed kale leaves

3 tablespoons olive oil

½ garlic clove

Pinch of sea salt or Sea Veg

PIZZA:

2 teaspoons olive oil, divided

1 pound store-bought pizza dough, cut in half (see note on page 126)

¾ cup shredded nondairy cheese

½ cup lightly packed arugula

Juice from ¼ lemon

Pinch of sea salt or Sea Veg

¼ avocado, pitted, peeled, and cubed

Snacks

Nana's Rolls, My Way ✈

YIELD: 9 ROLLS Bread, in any format, doesn't have a great reputation as a health food, mostly due to the low-carb craze. Still, we love bread and I wanted to figure out how to make my Nana's delicious rolls healthier. In fact, I think these are the only "rolls" that I feel pretty good about eating and serving. Enjoy, and love the fact that at least you're eating something healthier!

---

3 cups spelt flour

1 teaspoon sea salt or Sea Veg

¼ cup maple syrup

1 ¼-ounce packet or 2¼ teaspoons active dry yeast

¾ cup water

¼ cup olive oil, plus more for the bowl and baking dish

2 tablespoons powdered egg replacer plus ½ cup water, whisked together

COOK'S NOTES

1. In a medium bowl, add the spelt flour, sea salt, maple syrup, and yeast. Using a whisk or handheld electric mixer, set on low, mix until ingredients are combined.

2. In a small saucepan set over medium-low heat, combine the water and oil. Bring the water temperature to 130 degrees F or until very hot. Pour the warmed water mixture into the flour mixture and mix on low speed until all of the ingredients are combined. Pour in the egg-replacer mixture, mix on medium-high speed, and knead just until combined. Transfer the dough out onto a floured work surface and knead for 10 to 12 minutes until soft and elastic. Transfer to bowl and cover with a clean kitchen towel to rest for 10 minutes.

3. Uncover the bowl and transfer the dough to a clean and lightly greased (I like using olive oil) large bowl. Cover the bowl with a kitchen towel and allow the dough to rise in a draft-free part of your house, until it has doubled in size, about 1 hour. Remove the towel and transfer the dough to a lightly floured work surface. Knead the dough a few times and then immediately press it into a 1-inch-thick square. Cut the dough into 9 equally sized pieces and transfer them to a lightly greased 9 × 9-inch baking dish. Cover with a clean kitchen towel and allow to rise once more, until doubled in size, about 1 hour. Meanwhile, preheat oven to 350 degrees F.

4. Transfer the baking dish to the oven and bake until the rolls are lightly browned on the top, about 30 minutes. Allow to come to room temperature before pulling apart.

Shut Up and Listen

My extraordinary, long-lived Nana has no health issues. She lives and cooks alone, and she says she wants the type of food that she grew up on: farm to table. It is not a new way of eating, but it is a forgotten way of eating—we are trying to make farm to table relevant again. When she cooks today, Nana says she still wants food that is nutritious, easy, and filling. If she still desires that at ninety-three, she must be doing something right. Nana says it's all about home cooking, and that is why I say "shut up and cook."

INTUITIVE MOMENTS

My grandmother, Nana, is ninety-three years old (hopefully ninety-four by the time you read this), and she still makes the most magical rolls. They're so good they've become legendary to family and friends. My mother grew up with them. I grew up with them. My sisters and cousins grew up with them. Nana knows how much everyone loves her rolls. She knows they were part of our childhood. In fact, she'll still call and ask if I'd like her to send me some rolls. I guess the desire to give your loved ones your very best—showing your love through cooking—never goes away.

I wanted to do the same for my children. I wanted them to experience Nana's rolls, but I knew they couldn't tolerate some of the ingredients. I wondered how I could create these scrumptious rolls so my kids could eat and enjoy them without a reaction. Well, it took me a while, but I did it. Note that these are best if you eat them the same day you make them.

Toasted Nori and Sea Salt Popcorn ✈

SERVES 4 Movie night just got healthier. Seriously, why not get lost in your favorite love story while you show a little love to yourself, your friends, and your family by making popcorn a nutritional benefit?

---

1 teaspoon coconut oil plus 1 tablespoon melted coconut oil

½ cup popcorn kernels

1 tablespoon minced nori (½ sheet)

1 teaspoon nutritional yeast

Pinch of sea salt or Sea Veg

1. In a medium sauté pan set over medium heat, add 1 teaspoon coconut oil. When the oil is hot, add the popcorn kernels and immediately cover. When you hear the first kernel pop, you'll know it's starting to cook. Give the pan a shake every so often, until most of the kernels have popped.

2. Transfer the popcorn to a large bowl and toss with 1 tablespoon melted coconut oil, nori, nutritional yeast, and sea salt or Sea Veg.

Did You Know?

Simple, clean eating is healthy.

COOK'S NOTES

Double-Dip Black Bean Dip

SERVES 4 TO 6 We don't often associate snacking with health. But let's face it, we all love to snack, and we often feel like our options are limited when it comes to finding healthy snack foods. Dips are a great way to complement any snack food, and they're also a great way to add nutrients to even the most unhealthy snacks. Did I mention I love black beans?

---

1. In a blender, add the apple cider vinegar, water, yellow onion, garlic clove, black beans, sea salt or Sea Veg, cumin, and cilantro leaves; puree until smooth, about 1 minute, scraping down the sides of the blender if needed. If you'd like it thinner, feel free to add an additional splash of water or bean liquid. Serve alongside celery or carrot sticks. This dip can also be used as a condiment on pita or in a gluten-free wrap.

2 teaspoons apple cider vinegar

3 tablespoons water or cooking liquid from the beans

¼ yellow onion

1 garlic clove

1½ cups black beans (recipe on page 55)

½ teaspoon sea salt or Sea Veg

¼ teaspoon cumin

⅓ cup packed cilantro leaves

COOK'S NOTES

Garlic Boost Spread

SERVES 2 TO 4 You gotta love garlic! Garlic boosts the immune system and fights many diseases. Here is a way to get more garlic in your diet that is not overpowering (as if I need to twist your arm, because garlic tastes so good).

---

6 heads of garlic

2 tablespoons olive oil

1 teaspoon sea salt or Sea Veg

Crackers, to serve

Shut Up and Listen

A small change in your diet can make a lifetime's impact on your health. Try setting small goals and adding new changes to your meals; after all, what do you have to lose? And, more importantly, what do you have to gain from that small change? Good health!

1. Preheat oven to 400 degrees F. Slice off the tops of the garlic heads and remove any loose peel from the exterior of the garlic. Transfer the garlic to a small baking dish and drizzle the tops with the olive oil and sea salt or Sea Veg. Cover with foil and transfer to the oven to roast for 45 minutes to 1 hour, until very fragrant and softened. Remove from the oven, uncover, and allow to stand so it's cool enough to handle, about 15 minutes.

2. Push the garlic cloves from the head and into a small bowl. Using a fork, mash the garlic so it resembles more of a paste. Adjust the salt according to taste. Spread on your favorite crackers and enjoy!

COOK'S NOTES

Gypsy Girl Guacamole

SERVES 4 You probably know a lot of people who could dive into a bowl of great guacamole and live there until it's devoured. I know I could. Plus, the good fat from the avocado adds a nutritional powerhouse punch to snacking.

1. In a medium bowl, add the avocados. Using a fork, mash the avocados until mostly smooth. Fold in the cherry tomatoes, red onion, cilantro leaves, lime juice, and sea salt or Sea Veg. Serve alongside chips.

2 avocados, pitted, peeled, and halved

3 cherry tomatoes, finely diced

2 tablespoons red onion, finely minced

2 tablespoons cilantro leaves, minced

Juice from 2 limes

½ teaspoon sea salt or Sea Veg

Tortilla chips of your choice, for serving

COOK'S NOTES

Sweet Potato Fries with Rosemary

SERVES 4 Healthier fries? Can it be true? And can they be delicious? Because white potatoes are a nightshade vegetable (nightshades are believed to have a negative effect on nerve, muscle, digestion, and joint functions for some), I prefer using sweet potatoes.

1. Preheat oven to 400 degrees F. Line a baking sheet with parchment paper. Add the sweet potatoes and drizzle with the olive oil. Add the sprigs of rosemary and toss the sweet potatoes until they're thoroughly coated. Transfer to the oven to bake for 25 to 30 minutes, until the potatoes are tender when poked with a fork.

2 sweet potatoes, cut into 1-inch matchsticks

1 tablespoon olive oil

3 sprigs rosemary, leaves removed

COOK'S NOTES

INTUITIVE MOMENTS

In recent years, sweet potato fries have seemingly taken the world by storm at our favorite restaurants. Of course, I've been eating homemade fries since I was a little kid—but white potato fries. Realizing that all kids, and most adults, love French fries, I started making homemade sweet potato fries (on a tip from my mother who was always ahead of her time) because they are more nutritious. I add rosemary for a flavor boost, and bake instead of fry for a healthier version of America's favorite side dish or snack.

Parsnip Fries

SERVES 4 I bet you've never dreamed of parsnips as a party pleaser! These delicious fries will surely be a snack favorite and a healthy addition to your diet. Root vegetables like parsnips provide us with fiber and great phytonutrients, minerals, and vitamins.

3 to 4 small parsnips (about 1 pound), peeled and cut into matchsticks

1 tablespoon olive oil

½ teaspoon sea salt or Sea Veg

1 tablespoon fresh Italian parsley, minced

1. Preheat oven to 400 degrees F. On a parchment-lined baking sheet, toss the parsnips with the olive oil and sea salt or Sea Veg. Transfer to the oven to bake for 20 minutes; then add parsley and bake for an additional 20 minutes.

COOK'S NOTES

Honeymoon Salsa

SERVES 4 The best salsa doesn't come from a jar. It comes from your own two hands and your heart! Anything homemade is always my first choice to serve my family, even when it's this easy. Get fresh with this spicy salsa, which is loaded with vitamins and nutrients.

1. Combine all of the ingredients in a medium bowl. Give it a taste and adjust the salt according to your liking. Serve immediately with chips, or you can cover with plastic wrap and transfer to the fridge to chill.

- 4 vine-ripe tomatoes, finely chopped
- ¼ cup onion, finely minced
- ¼ cup cilantro, finely minced
- ½ serrano pepper, seeded and finely minced
- ½ jalapeño pepper, seeded and finely minced
- Juice from ½ lime
- ½ teaspoon sea salt or Sea Veg
- Tortilla chips of your choice, to serve

COOK'S NOTES

Did You Know?

Home cooking has a profound impact on your health—simply because you know what you're eating.

INTUITIVE MOMENTS

Many years ago, I took my husband on a surprise trip to Tulum, Mexico, for our anniversary. We loved the music, the culture, the weather, and especially the food. Oh my gosh—talk about fresh tomatoes! While we were there, we decided to take a cooking class. I learned a lot. But what truly surprised me was just how easy it is to make fresh, spicy, healthy salsa from scratch. I like to add jalapeño and serrano peppers. For those of you who are truly bold and love the heat, try adding a habañero. But don't hold me responsible if your tongue catches on fire! This salsa is great with chips or the Huevos Rancheros on page 34.

Modern Focaccia Bread ✈

SERVES 4 Easy, breezy, and tasty! You can bake up your own focaccia bread in an instant. The added herbs in this recipe make this a truly sensational addition to any meal as a side. I like to make it myself, surprising those at my table with a healthy version.

---

1. Preheat oven to 400 degrees F. In a 10-inch cast-iron skillet rubbed with 1 teaspoon olive oil, stretch out the ball of pizza dough, pressing it until it completely covers the bottom and reaches the inside edge of the pan. Using your fingers, press into the dough, creating craters. Drizzle the olive oil on top of the dough. Sprinkle the dough with the Italian seasoning, rosemary leaves, and a pinch of sea salt or Sea Veg. Transfer to the oven to bake until golden brown, about 15 to 20 minutes.

1 pound store-bought pizza dough (see note on page 126)

1 tablespoon plus 1 teaspoon of olive oil, divided

2 teaspoons Italian seasoning

1 sprig of fresh rosemary, leaves removed

¼ teaspoon sea salt or Sea Veg

COOK'S NOTES

INTUITIVE MOMENTS

One day I was making Chicken in the Garden (my husband's favorite dish), and I wished I could make some homemade bread—for a complete home-style meal. Of course, I didn't have time to make bread from scratch. I did have frozen pizza dough in the freezer though, and I knew that it could be thawed in a couple hours. That could be quick and easy. But how could I make it delicious so it wasn't just plain, boring bread? Restaurant bread always has a shiny, golden appeal. I drizzled olive oil over the top to bake it to golden perfection. Then I sprinkled on some fresh rosemary, Italian seasoning, and Sea Veg for some extra kick. What started as a simple thought has now become a family favorite. We don't eat this often, but when we do, it is appreciated, loved, and devoured. Plus, it takes very little time or effort.

Chips ✈

The potato has monopolized the chip world for far too long. It's time to get some nutrition from our favorite snack foods. Chips—made at home with love!

ZUCCHINI CHIPS

SERVES 1 TO 2

½ zucchini, very
thinly sliced

1 teaspoon olive oil

Pinch of sea salt
or Sea Veg

1. Preheat oven to 250 degrees F. Line a baking sheet with a piece of parchment paper. Place the zucchini slices side by side, being sure to not overlap them. Pour olive oil in a bowl and brush each slice (one side only) of zucchini with olive oil. Sprinkle the slices with sea salt or Sea Veg and transfer to the oven to bake for 1 hour.

2. At the 1-hour mark, turn the heat down to 200 degrees F and bake for an additional hour. Remove from the oven and allow the chips to cool to room temperature. Repeat these steps if you desire more to nibble on. Delicious! *Bon appétit.*

MUSHROOM CHIPS

SERVES 1 TO 2

8 to 10 uncut shiitake
mushrooms

½ teaspoon olive
oil, divided

Pinch of sea salt
or Sea Veg

1. Preheat oven to 400 degrees F. Line a baking sheet with a piece of parchment paper. Slice the shiitake mushrooms lengthwise. Drizzle about ¼ teaspoon of olive oil onto the baking sheet. Add the mushrooms and rub them around in the olive oil. Transfer to the oven to bake for 15 to 20 minutes.

2. Remove the baking sheet from the oven and drizzle with an additional ¼ teaspoon olive oil and a few pinches of sea salt or Sea Veg; toss one last time. Great to eat on their own or as an addition to Soothing Butternut Soup (recipe on page 123).

INTUITIVE MOMENTS

Snack attack, beware! Making chips from your favorite vegetables lets you have a crazy good time minimizing the munchies. Using thinly sliced veggies, this cooking process is a lot like dehydrating. These chips become crunchy and delicious. They're perfect after school, at a desk, or in front of the television while watching your favorite show. They're oh so tasty and oh so good. After all, you're consuming vegetables, so guilt can sit on the sidelines.

BRUSSELS SPROUTS CHIPS

1. Preheat oven to 275 degrees F. Line a baking sheet with a piece of parchment paper. Trim off the ends of the brussels sprouts and then separate the leaves. Toss the leaves with sea salt and olive oil on the baking sheet, and then spread the leaves in an even layer so they do not overlap on the sheet. Transfer to the oven to bake for 15 to 20 minutes, until crispy. Remove from the oven and allow to cool to room temperature before serving.

SERVES 1 TO 2

5 brussels sprouts

Pinch of sea salt or Sea Veg

½ teaspoon olive oil

BEET CHIPS

1. Preheat oven to 250 degrees F. Line a baking sheet with a piece of parchment paper. Slice the beet thinly using a mandoline or a sharp knife. I like to get them super thin, which is why I prefer the mandoline, but be careful if you use one because the blade is super sharp.

2. Pour the olive oil in a small bowl.

3. Place the beet slices side by side on the baking sheet, being sure to not overlap them. Brush the beet slices on both sides with a bit of olive oil, being sure to not oversaturate them as this will result in chewy beets rather than crispy chips. Transfer to the oven to bake for about 1 hour. Check their crispiness periodically. Remove from the oven to cool to room temperature; they'll become crunchier as they cool. Top with a pinch of sea salt or Sea Veg.

SERVES 1 TO 2

1 beet

1 teaspoon olive oil

Pinch of sea salt or Sea Veg

COOK'S NOTES

French-Style Radishes with Nondairy Butter

SERVES 4 You do not have to be French to enjoy this famous French ensemble. More people can enjoy this classic dish if you prepare it with a nondairy butter. I bet you never dreamed radishes could taste so good!

6 radishes

1 teaspoon large flaked sea salt (such as Maldon®)

1 stick (¼ cup) nondairy butter, softened

¼ cup chives, thinly chopped

1 teaspoon sea salt or Sea Veg

1. Put the radishes and sea salt on a plate.

2. Place softened nondairy butter, chopped chives, and sea salt or Sea Veg in a small bowl and combine using a rubber spatula.

3. Serve as dip with the radishes or roll into a log, cover with plastic wrap, and refrigerate for future use.

COOK'S NOTES

Desserts

INTUITIVE MOMENTS

We all have a sweet tooth. The question isn't whether we give up the sweets. The question is how can we satisfy our sweet desires without consuming too many unhealthy ingredients or experiencing negative health effects? Or, even better, how can we add healthy ingredients to our sweets so that they're actually a bit beneficial for us to eat?

I didn't invent this recipe, although I seriously thought I was the first to come up with it. I woke up early one morning before a charity bike ride and thought, "How can I make something sweet for my kids before I leave the house?" I had also heard many people say that they like sweetness with salt. I wondered what it would taste like to make homemade kale chips, add them to my cookie batter, and bake. Of course, I also thought that it was just a crazy idea and the cookies would surely turn out gross. But I had to try it. To my surprise, people love them!

Even though people had been making kale chip cookies for a long time, I thought I was inventive—and I guess I was because I'd never looked to see if it had been done before. I just got in the kitchen and did it. In fact, I took cookies with me to the event that morning and gave them to my friends . . . and they loved them, too. They asked for more after they guessed what was in them.

Chocolate Chip Cookies with Crispy Kale ✈

YIELD: 12 COOKIES A cookie with kale? Yep, you read that right. How often have you wondered why the best-tasting foods can't be healthier? I used to wonder that. This strangely delicious recipe offers the sweetness you expect with a bit of saltiness and all the health benefits of kale. I was *shocked* that my kids and friends would love cookies with this unlikely ingredient!

1. Preheat oven to 350 degrees F. Line a baking sheet with parchment paper. On the baking sheet, toss the kale leaves in the olive oil and pinch of sea salt or Sea Veg. Spread the leaves out on the baking sheet so they're in one layer. Transfer to the oven to bake until crispy, about 10 to 15 minutes. Allow to cool completely on the baking sheet; they'll become crispier as they cool.

2. Meanwhile, in a large bowl, whisk together the brown rice flour, garbanzo fava flour, baking powder, and a pinch of salt or Sea Veg. In a medium bowl, whisk together the applesauce, maple syrup, coconut oil, apple cider vinegar, and pure vanilla extract. In one batch, pour the wet ingredients into the dry ingredients and mix until combined. Fold in the chocolate chips and kale chips. As you mix them in, the kale chips will break apart a bit—that's OK!

3. Line two baking sheets with parchment paper. Scoop out balls of cookie dough and drop them onto the baking sheet, spacing them about 2 inches apart. Transfer to the oven to bake for 12 to 15 minutes, until the edges are lightly golden brown. Allow to cool to room temperature before serving.

1½ cups lightly packed kale leaves

1 teaspoon olive oil

Pinches sea salt or Sea Veg

¾ cups brown rice flour

1½ cups garbanzo fava flour

1½ teaspoons baking powder

½ teaspoon baking soda

½ cup applesauce

½ cup maple syrup

¼ cup melted coconut oil

1 teaspoon apple cider vinegar

1 teaspoon pure vanilla extract

1 cup nondairy chocolate chips or chocolate chips of your choice

COOK'S NOTES

Grandma's Nondairy Sweet Potato Pie ✈

SERVES 8 Traditions don't need to die simply because you want to eat healthier. Altering my grandma's traditional recipe into a healthier version provides a delectable option that's wonderful any time of year. But this pie is especially great to make and serve, or to bring as a treat, during the holidays to share with your loved ones.

2 cups (from 1 pound) sweet potatoes, cubed

½ cup rice milk

½ cup maple syrup

3 tablespoons tapioca starch

1 teaspoon ground cinnamon

¼ teaspoon ground ginger

Pinch ground cloves

Pinch nutmeg

1 nondairy store-bought pie crust

1. Bring a medium pot filled with water to a boil. Add the cubed sweet potatoes and boil until tender, about 10 minutes.

2. Preheat oven to 375 degrees F. Drain the cooked sweet potato and transfer to a medium bowl, along with the rice milk, maple syrup, tapioca starch, cinnamon, ginger, cloves, and nutmeg. Stir vigorously until the mixture is very smooth. Pour the filling into the prepared pie crust.

3. Transfer to the oven to bake for 40 minutes, until the edges are golden brown and the center has set completely. Cool for at least 15 to 20 minutes before slicing into the pie.

COOK'S NOTES

INTUITIVE MOMENTS

We all have those special memories from childhood—often times relating to food that only a grandmother can create with love. My dad's mother lives in Cleveland, Ohio. And, oh, how I remember her homemade sweet potato pie. It was so good—and it's what I recall every time I think of Cleveland. In fact, I believe it was the only pie I ever ate growing up. It was the first thing I would ask Grandma for when we would visit Ohio in the summer months: "I love you. How are you? Did you make sweet potato pie?"

This pie was so decadent; it was divine. And it was jam-packed with butter and sugar and all the ingredients I spend so much time avoiding now. It took me a while to create, but this recipe will surprise and delight you. In fact, it's so good that your second slice might be even more satisfying than your first!

Guilt-Free Doughnuts

YIELD: 12 DOUGHNUTS OK, so maybe there will never be a healthy doughnut. But that doesn't mean we can't create a healthier version of one of our favorite treats. I never feel guilty eating these doughnuts because I know how they were made and the ingredients I used to make them—healthier alternatives and a whole lotta love.

DOUGHNUTS:

1 teaspoon coconut oil or olive oil, for doughnut pan

2¼ cups spelt flour

2 teaspoons baking powder

1 tablespoon powdered egg replacer

3 tablespoons water

2 tablespoons olive oil

1 cup rice milk

⅓ cup agave

CHOCOLATE GLAZE:

4 tablespoons maple syrup

4 tablespoons cacao powder

2 teaspoons pure vanilla extract

1. Preheat oven to 350 degrees F. Rub the six cavities in the doughnut pan with coconut oil or olive oil. Set aside.

2. In a medium bowl, whisk together the spelt flour and baking powder. In another medium bowl, whisk together the powdered egg replacer with three tablespoons of water. Next, whisk in the olive oil, rice milk, and agave. In one batch, add the wet ingredients to the dry and mix until just combined.

3. Distribute half of the batter to the cavities in the doughnut pan. Transfer to the oven to bake for 9 to 10 minutes, until lightly golden brown. Remove from the doughnut pan by running a butter knife alongside the edges—they should pop right out! Repeat the greasing, filling, and baking steps with the remaining batter.

4. In the meantime, make the glaze. In a small bowl whisk together the maple syrup, cacao powder, and pure vanilla extract. Dip the cooled doughnuts in the glaze before serving. These are best consumed fresh, the day you make them.

Shut Up and Listen

Sugar is in most of the processed foods in America. Although it's tough to avoid it altogether, you don't have to make sugar your best friend—try to avoid it when you can. I created these recipes without using sugar, and so can you.

COOK'S NOTES

Watermelon Granita

SERVES 6 TO 8 This summertime delight is quite possibly the most refreshing thing you'll ever taste. Jam-packed with vitamin A, vitamin C, antioxidants, and some amino acids, this recipe is great for cooling off on a hot day, or as a surprise treat for guests.

1. Depending on the size of your blender, you may need to do this in batches. Add the watermelon, maple syrup, and lime juice to the blender jar. Pulse until smooth, about 30 seconds. Pour the watermelon puree into an 8 × 8-inch baking dish. Cover with plastic wrap and transfer to the freezer for 2 hours.

2. At the 2-hour mark, remove the baking dish from the freezer and scrape at the surface of the frozen watermelon mixture using a fork, until it resembles a slushy. Return the baking dish (no need to transfer it to another dish) to the freezer to freeze one last time, about 2 additional hours. Just before serving, scrape the entire granita. Divide between the bowls and garnish with fresh mint leaves before serving. Store in the freezer, in a freezer-safe container, for up to 2 weeks.

1 seedless watermelon (about 4½ pounds), peeled and chopped

2 tablespoons maple syrup

Juice from 1 lime

Fresh mint, for garnish

COOK'S NOTES

Nondairy Strawberry Ice Cream

YIELD: 1½ PINTS There's nothing more rewarding on a hot summer day than a scoop of your favorite flavor of ice cream. The sad thing, however, is that it's often sprinkled with guilt and can give people with dairy sensitivity a bad experience. This dairy-free and delicious recipe is tolerable to even the most finicky stomach, and it can be enjoyed by everyone without guilt. Serve it up!

1 pound fresh strawberries, rinsed and hulled

1 cup full-fat coconut milk

⅓ cup maple syrup

1 teaspoon pure vanilla extract

Special equipment: Ice cream maker

1. In a blender, add the strawberries, coconut milk, maple syrup, and pure vanilla extract, and pulse until smooth, about 30 seconds. Transfer the blender jar with the mixture (alternatively you could transfer it to a glass bowl and cover it) to the fridge and chill for at least 2 hours.

2. Pour the strawberry mixture into the ice cream maker bowl and churn according to your ice cream maker's instructions. Serve immediately for soft serve, or you can transfer it to a freezer-safe container and freeze for at least 4 hours. Store in the freezer for up to 2 to 3 weeks.

COOK'S NOTES

INTUITIVE MOMENTS

Yes, at one time, I seriously considered going into the ice cream business. I was passionate about creating vegan ice cream because I had a child who couldn't eat dairy-based ice cream. You couldn't find vegan ice cream back then. Why should one of my kids be able to enjoy ice cream if the other couldn't?

I remember my grandmother making homemade ice cream and asking me if I wanted to lick the spoon as she made it. And I loved it. Kids love ice cream. I didn't want my kids to be deprived.

For a while, I partnered with a chef to create something special. That business never came to fruition. Here is a different version that I've tweaked a few times. It's so good that you'll wonder how this is even possible. In fact, make some for your next dinner party. You'll get a kick out of how many guests will rave about it and think they should feel guilty about eating your totally nutritious dessert.

Did You Know?

Certain food dyes have been found to cause children to be hyperactive. Is adding particular colors worth it? Mother earth does not need help from dyes.

Pineapple Lemon Granita

SERVES 4 Share a flare of the islands with this delicious dessert. Fiber, minerals, and vitamins make this recipe a delightful boost to your diet. How often can you say that about dessert? That's why you'll absolutely love this granita!

---

1 pineapple (about 2 pounds), peeled and chopped

Juice from ½ lemon

Did You Know?

"GMO" means Genetically Modified Organisms, foods that have been tampered with using genetic engineering (for example, crops that have been altered to make them resistant to parasites).

1. Depending on the size of your blender, you may need to do this in batches. Add the pineapple and lemon juice to the blender jar. Pulse until smooth, about 30 seconds. Pour the pineapple puree into an 8 × 8-inch baking dish. Cover with plastic wrap and transfer to the freezer for 2 hours.

2. At the 2-hour mark, remove the baking dish from the freezer and scrape the surface using a fork. Return the baking dish (no need to transfer it to another dish) to the freezer to freeze one last time, 2 additional hours. Just before serving, scrape the entire granita. Divide between four bowls and serve. Store in the freezer, in a freezer-safe container, for up to 2 weeks.

COOK'S NOTES

Childhood Bundt Cake

YIELD: 1 (8-INCH) BUNDT CAKE The goal is to enjoy the foods we love but in healthier formats. This recipe is a bit more wholesome than the original recipe but still tastes just as good, if not better!

1. Preheat oven to 325 degrees F. Grease bundt pan with a tablespoon of margarine and set aside. In a medium bowl, add the spelt flour, baking powder, and baking soda. In a measuring cup, whisk together the rice milk and sparkling water. Set aside.

2. In a medium bowl, whisk together the egg replacer with the water. Using a hand mixer, on medium speed, beat the remaining margarine and maple syrup together until soft and creamy, about 3 to 4 minutes. Pour in the egg replacer mixture and add the lemon zest, lime zest, and pure vanilla extract. Next, add the rice milk mixture and flour mixture, alternating between the two and stirring until no flour speckles are visible.

3. Pour into the greased bundt pan and bake for 45 to 55 minutes until a skewer or a toothpick comes out clean.

4. To make the glaze, whisk all ingredients together and drizzle over cake. Transfer cake to the refrigerator until glaze hardens, about 20 minutes.

CAKE:

¾ cup nondairy margarine, softened (I used Earth Balance Vegan Buttery Sticks®), plus 1 tablespoon for bundt pan

4 cups spelt flour

2 teaspoons baking powder

½ teaspoon baking soda

¼ cup unsweetened rice milk

¼ cup sparkling water

4 tablespoons powdered egg replacer

12 tablespoons water

1¼ cups maple syrup

Zest from 1 lemon (about 1 tablespoon)

Zest from 1 lime (about 1 teaspoon)

2 teaspoons pure vanilla extract

LEMON GLAZE:

⅓ cup melted coconut oil

2 tablespoons maple syrup

Zest from 1 lemon

Juice from ½ lemon

COOK'S NOTES

INTUITIVE MOMENTS

Everyone loves a mystery . . . unless, of course, you're eating one. As a child I remember my aunt making the most fabulous 7Up bundt cake. I don't know how she made it or all the ingredients she used because she passed away when I was young. I was never able to ask, but I remember it was delicious, and I wondered if I could create the same thing, except healthier.

This recipe is a perfect dessert for your dinner parties or holiday gatherings, or just as a treat to satisfy your sweet tooth or your family's urge to splurge.

Did You Know?

Many recent studies suggest that sugar is addictive. However, you don't have to deprive yourself of delicious desserts. Choose a healthy alternative like this recipe.

Scrumptious Sweet Apple Pie ✈

YIELD: 1 (9-INCH) PIE The all-time American favorite just got better, healthier, more modern, and tolerable for people who live with dietary restrictions. It cannot get easier than this. And the taste? Forget about it! It's delicious!

1. Preheat oven to 400 degrees F. In a medium bowl, toss the apples with the maple syrup, pure vanilla extract, cinnamon, cloves, and allspice. Pour the apple mixture into the first nondairy pie crust tin. Place the second pie crust, upside down, on top and gently loosen it from its tin. Press the edges of the pie crust, securing the top and bottom crusts, and make small slits with a knife in the top part of the pie dough. Transfer to the oven to bake for 30 minutes. At the 30-minute mark, turn the heat down to 300 degrees F and bake for an additional 30 minutes.

2. Remove from the oven and allow to cool for 10 to 15 minutes before slicing.

1½ pounds apples, cored and cut into slices

2 tablespoons maple syrup

1 teaspoon pure vanilla extract

1 teaspoon ground cinnamon

Pinch of ground cloves

Pinch of allspice

2 store-bought nondairy pie crusts, in their tins

COOK'S NOTES

INTUITIVE MOMENTS

I didn't grow up eating apple pie. But I did grow up eating sautéed apples that my mom used to make, and I thought my kids would like apple pie. When I made the first apple pie that my son could eat, his eyes were fixated on it. They were three times their normal size and bulging out of their sockets. The pie was oozing and gooey with a perfectly golden brown crust. And, he dug in like I had never seen him do before.

In this recipe, I use store-bought pie crusts and fill them with my mom's homemade cinnamon-apple recipe. I make this every holiday and no one can believe that there's no milk, butter, eggs, or sugar in the mixture. It's not just for people with dietary restrictions—this is simply a healthier option than traditional apple pie.

Soy Butter Rice Krispies® Cups

YIELD: 8 TO 10 CUPS Everyone loves the classic Rice Krispies treats. Kids love them. Adults love them (even if they don't admit it). This recipe is a great alternative, with a cocoa twist, for people who may have allergies or sensitivities to the traditional treats. They're perfect for anyone who wants some good-ole simple and scrumptious candy made with love.

¼ cup baking cocoa powder

¼ cup creamy soy nut butter

3 tablespoons maple syrup

½ teaspoon pure vanilla extract

¼ cup coconut oil, melted and warm

¼ cup crispy brown rice cereal

1. In a medium bowl, add the cocoa powder, soy butter, maple syrup, pure vanilla extract, and coconut oil. Mix until very smooth. If the mixture is at all dry, add an additional teaspoon of warm coconut oil.

2. Next, fold in the crispy brown rice cereal and divide among 8 to 10 mini cupcake liners. Transfer to the freezer to set for about 30 minutes. These melt easily so keep them in the freezer until you're ready to serve.

> **Did You Know?**
>
> *Many packaged foods contain chemicals so that they appear to be "fresh" when you want to eat them. How fresh are chemicals? Try to look for an organic alternative if you must use a packaged product.*

INTUITIVE MOMENTS

Candy doesn't have to makes us feel horrible. In fact, it brings little smiles to our faces, even when it isn't filled with things we shouldn't eat. As a kid, I used to love peanut butter cups. I still do, but out of respect for my kids' dietary restrictions, I don't eat them anymore. One day at the grocery store, I thought, "I want to make my kids candy." I looked at the peanut butter cup wrapper and, of course, it was loaded with all the things they can't eat. But I knew I could come up with something.

Instead of buying a bunch of new ingredients, I thought I would go back home, check the pantry, and see what I could create with ingredients I already had. Within minutes, I had discovered just how many sweet, delicious ingredients were already in my cabinets—I could use cocoa for chocolate and soy butter instead of nut butter. The only problem, of course, was that my candy didn't hold together like the stuff you find at the checkout counter. No problem—I just put in the freezer. And what a surprise: It was cold. It was crisp. And, it tasted like it was meant to. You need to keep these in the freezer. Not only does the cold hold them together, but it actually accentuates the flavor (after two weeks they will still taste fresh).

Don't be afraid to experiment in your kitchen. Some of the most amazing and delectable treats can be made from the ingredients you already have in your cupboards.

COOK'S NOTES

Cinnamon Saturday Apple Crisp

YIELD: ABOUT 15 TO 20 CRISPS Among the benefits you'll quickly discover about cooking at home are the wonderful aromas that will fill the air—especially when you try this recipe. The smell of this apple crisp warms my home and makes us eager to devour these delicious treats. Apples and cinnamon offer numerous health benefits, too!

1. Preheat oven to 250 degrees F. Line a baking sheet with parchment paper. Set aside.

2. I love using my mandoline to slice the apple—it gets them nice and thin. If you don't have one, use a good, sharp knife to slice the rounds very thinly. Just be careful not to cut yourself. Slice the entire apple into rounds. Place the apple slices side by side onto the parchment-lined baking sheet, being sure they do not overlap.

3. In a bowl, mix together the syrup and cinnamon. Brush the apple rounds on both sides with the syrup and cinnamon mixture. Transfer the rounds to the baking sheet and bake for 1 hour. At the 1-hour mark, remove the baking sheet from the oven and flip the apple rounds over. Turn the oven down to 200 degrees F and bake for an additional hour. Remove the apples from the oven and allow to cool. They'll get crispier as they cool. Sprinkle a little bit more cinnamon on top of the apple slices.

4. Repeat these steps for more apple crisps if desired. If the apples are not completely crispy, it means they were sliced a bit too thick. Keep in mind, the thinner, the crispier! These apples will make your house smell so delicious and yummy. Be sure to eat them alongside a warm cup of **tea** or **apple cider**.

1 apple (Honeycrisp is my favorite), unpeeled

1 tablespoon maple syrup

½ teaspoon ground cinnamon, plus more for garnish

COOK'S NOTES

INTUITIVE MOMENTS

I remember taking an autumn field trip as a kid. We loaded on and off that big yellow school bus. We gazed at the changing leaves—the brilliant fall colors that had been touched by Mother Nature. I distinctly recall the chill in the air and the realization that it was fall, and that Halloween was coming.

Remembering that day like it was yesterday, I found myself one autumn afternoon wanting to re-create the warmth of apple crisps for my kids. The problem was that I only had a few large green apples in the house. I wondered what would happen if I baked them. The result was this wonderful snack.

This recipe will surely become a family favorite—as a snack for kids and for adults, for that cozy feeling. These apple chips warm the heart and soul. They might bring you back in time as well—to a day you felt the chill of winter approaching, and the warmth of a cinnamon snack.

Vegan Cheesecake

Don't run at the sight of "vegan cheesecake"—shut up and cook! This recipe, my friends, is going to surprise everyone. I swear by it! My mother made the best cheese-cake I ever had, but because I changed my way of eating, this recipe was born. The fresh strawberries and the alternative cake ingredients are a wonderful combination and a great option for a much healthier version than traditional cheesecake.

CRUST:

1¼ cup graham cracker crumbs

1 teaspoon ground cinnamon

¼ cup nondairy butter, melted

CHEESECAKE:

¾ cup plus 1 tablespoon maple syrup

¾ cup vegan sour cream

¼ cup spelt flour

2 tablespoons rice milk

Zest from 1 lemon

Juice from ½ lemon

1 teaspoon pure vanilla extract

¼ teaspoon sea salt or Sea Veg

24 ounces soy Tofutti® cream cheese (from three 8-ounce containers), at room temperature

STRAWBERRY TOPPING:

3 cups strawberries, washed, stems removed, sliced

2 tablespoons maple syrup

Juice from ½ lemon

1. Preheat oven to 325 degrees F. Wrap the outside of a springform pan with aluminum foil and set aside.

2. In a medium bowl, combine graham cracker crumbs with cinnamon and butter, and stir to combine. Press crumb mixture evenly into the bottom of the springform pan.

3. In a medium bowl, add the maple syrup, sour cream, spelt flour, rice milk, lemon zest and juice, pure vanilla extract, and sea salt. Using an electric hand mixer on medium speed, beat until mixture is smooth and free of lumps.

4. In a separate medium bowl, add the cream cheese and beat with an electric hand mixer until very smooth.

5. Combine the beaten cream cheese and sour cream mixture, and beat once more until very smooth. Pour the filling into the springform pan.

6. Place a large baking dish in the preheated oven and add the springform pan to the center of the dish. Pour 1 cup of boiling water into the baking dish. The steam from the water will ensure that the cheesecake stays moist and will prevent the top from cracking.

6. Bake the cheesecake for 1½ hours. Remove from oven and let cool completely. Once cooled, run a small spatula around the edges and transfer to the fridge overnight.

7. Before serving, make the strawberry topping by combining sliced strawberries with maple syrup and lemon juice. Let this mixture sit in the refrigerator for an hour before serving. Top the cheesecake with the strawberry mixture; slice and serve.

COOK'S NOTES

Decadent Chocolate Truffles ✈

YIELD: 12 TRUFFLES For all you chocolate lovers of the world, here's a recipe that will allow you to indulge your cravings . . . at least a little. Again, homemade is always better!

5 ounces vegan chocolate chips

1 tablespoon maple syrup

1 teaspoon coconut oil

1 teaspoon pure vanilla extract

⅓ cup cocoa powder

1. Fill a saucepan with a few inches of water. Place a glass or stainless steel bowl atop the saucepan and set it over medium heat. Pour the chocolate chips into the bowl and allow to melt, about 2 minutes. Remove the bowl, being careful because it will be hot. Mix in maple syrup, coconut oil, and pure vanilla extract until very smooth. Cover the bowl with plastic wrap and transfer to the refrigerator to set, about 1 hour.

2. Pour cocoa powder into a shallow plate or bowl. Using a melon baller, scoop out balls of the chilled chocolate mixture and roll them into circles using your palms. Drop the chocolate balls into the cocoa powder and transfer them to a plate or mini cupcake liners. Repeat the process of scooping, forming, and rolling the remaining chocolate in cocoa powder. Transfer the chocolate truffles to an airtight container and place them in the fridge until you're ready to serve. Just a heads up—these truffles get melty when they're out for too long.

COOK'S NOTES

Balsamic Strawberries with Basil

SERVES 4 TO 6 This simple mix-up of fresh herbs and fruit will make you wonder why you don't combine these seemingly odd couplings more often. Loaded with antioxidants, this refreshing twist on dessert is quite possibly the simplest crowd-pleaser you'll ever create!

1. In a medium bowl, whisk together the vinegar and basil leaves. Add the strawberries and toss until the berries are evenly coated in the vinegar.

2 teaspoons
balsamic vinegar

2 tablespoons fresh
basil leaves, minced

1 pound strawberries,
stems removed and sliced

COOK'S NOTES

Raspberry Strawberry Soup

SERVES 4 Have you ever had fruit soup—as dessert? It's not common, but it may soon be, as you'll love this unique recipe that allows you and your family to get more of the vitamins and minerals you need in your diets. Loaded with antioxidants, this soup is a surprisingly sweet treat after any meal. Trust me on this one—your loved ones will eat it all up!

---

1 pound strawberries, stems removed

1½ cups (6 ounces) raspberries

½ cup rice milk

Fresh mint leaves, for garnish

1. In a blender, add the strawberries, raspberries, and rice milk. Pulse until smooth, about 30 seconds. Divide among four bowls and garnish with fresh mint leaves.

Did You Know?

Food is supposed to heal us and keep us healthy, not cause health problems.

COOK'S NOTES

INTUITIVE MOMENTS

If you have a blender, be extra careful about the buttons you push . . . or you just might create something extraordinary—like a dessert soup. Seriously, this recipe might be the outcome of fantastic mistake, but so were many things. Would anybody know about the Tower of Pisa if it wasn't leaning? Probably not. And I wouldn't have ever thought about creating a fantastically sweet and nutritious dessert soup unless I accidentally over-pureed my smoothie one day. Instantly, I realized I had created a beautiful dessert soup. Add a garnish, like fresh mint, and you've got a photo-worthy dish that will be admired by all.

Drinks

Green Juice

SERVES 2 This power drink is a serious one for the true health-minded "it just needs to taste good enough" individual. I love drinking my greens because I get a healthy, powerful variety of nutrition all at once. My kids stare as I consume!

3 bunches of collard green leaves, stems removed

1 lemon

2 large bunches of kale leaves, stems removed

1 handful parsley leaves

1 (2-inch) knob of ginger, peeled

½ teaspoon ground turmeric

Special equipment: Juicer

1. In a juicer, add the collard greens, lemon, kale leaves, parsley leaves, and ginger. Mix in the ground turmeric once all the items have been juiced. Give it a nice stir and then pour into two glasses.

COOK'S NOTES

Did You Know?

"Conventional" means a fruit, vegetable, or animal product that has been chemically treated, which may have an adverse reaction to someone's health.

Raspberry Sorbet with Sparkling Water

YIELD: 2 PINTS Specialty drinks aren't just for bartenders. This drink is a fantastic summertime cooler or a great pre-meal palette teaser! Plus, what more could you ask for than antioxidants infused into H2O? It's simply perfect.

1. In a medium saucepan, combine the water and maple syrup. Stir until the maple syrup dissolves, about a minute. Set aside to cool.

2. In a food processor or blender, add the maple syrup mixture, raspberries, and lime juice. Pulse until smooth. Run the raspberry puree through a strainer to remove the seeds. Pour the mixture into the ice cream maker and churn according to your maker's instructions. Eat right away for a very soft sorbet or transfer to a quart container and freeze for at least 8 hours. Keeps in the freezer for 2 to 3 weeks.

3. To make a sparkling water dessert, add a few scoops of sorbet to four glasses. Top with about 4 ounces each of sparkling water.

2 cups water

1 cup maple syrup

2 quarts raspberries, halved

2 tablespoons lime juice

16 ounces sparkling water, to serve

Special equipment: Ice cream maker

COOK'S NOTES

INTUITIVE MOMENTS

When I was growing up, on family birthdays, my mother would always make a special drink or punch for us. She would always add rainbow sherbet ice cream. It was delicious. I wanted the same for my family without the dairy.

This is pure refreshment on a summer day. Instead of grabbing one of those ice-swirled concoctions at your local corner store, try this quick and easy recipe that is sure to delight. The raspberry sorbet is light and cold—it's really sweet and really nutritious. Pour some sparkling water over the top and you'll find a summertime drink that can't be beat.

Cooling Watermelon Juice

SERVES 2 Watermelon is a summertime staple. In fact, it's almost as much a symbol of a hot, sunny day as a beach ball. This juice tastes like summertime in a glass. Because it's fresh and cooling beyond words can express, you'll love this beverage!

3 cups cubed watermelon (from about a 2-pound melon)

½ cup fresh or frozen raspberries

4 kiwis, peeled and cubed

½ lime, peeled

Special equipment: juicer

1. In a large bowl, combine the cubed watermelon, raspberries, cubed kiwi, and peeled lime. Turn your juicer on and add the fruit, in handfuls, to the juicer. Repeat until you've worked your way through all of the fruit.

2. If you don't own a juicer, you can use a blender. Add all of the ingredients to a blender, in batches, and squeeze in the lime juice. Pulse until smooth. Pour the juice through a strainer. Pour into two glasses.

Did You Know?

I used to have to take my kids to the doctor's office monthly because they got sick very often. Once I changed their diets, we now rarely need to go. Food heals or hurts—and we decide what to feed ourselves and our loved ones.

COOK'S NOTES

INTUITIVE MOMENTS

When I was pregnant, I craved watermelon. I blame a certain, and incredible, chef named Marcus Samuelsson at a fine restaurant, who once made me a salad that I thought, at the time (in the year 2000), was an odd combination of lettuce and watermelon. Something about that salad stuck with me. I couldn't stop thinking about it. Sure, it may have been a crazy pregnancy craving, but I wanted more watermelon. At the time, I wondered if I could juice watermelon—you know, get as much of it as possible in one serving. So I started testing. I kept testing. And it didn't take long until I discovered pure refreshment. I had created a watermelon juice that is simply irresistible—especially on a sunny day. And it was inspired by Marcus's salad!

Tropical Fruit Smoothie

SERVES 2 It's like a mini-vacation to an island paradise all in one glass—and plenty of vitamin C to keep you healthy and strong. This is a feel-good smoothie. Try it! Escape for a few minutes to your favorite beach.

---

1. In a blender, add the pineapple, mango, coconut water, and lime juice. Pulse until smooth, about 20 seconds. Pour into two glasses.

1 cup diced pineapple

1 cup diced mango

¾ cup coconut water

Juice from 1 lime

COOK'S NOTES

Shut Up and Listen

Why are we letting society dictate the size of our dinner plate? In Europe, the cups, bowls, and plates are half the size of their American counterparts. In the 1950s the American plate size was 9 inches. Today, it is 12 inches or more. That's more food on one plate, at one serving, not including going for seconds. One helpful suggestion I offer: Instead of drinking that orange juice in a large glass, reduce the glass size to half. If we can get real and honest, we need to think small—smaller plates, smaller glasses, and smaller serving sizes. Put your dinner on the salad plate and your salad on the dinner plate. You might be surprised that small servings seem much more satisfying.

Avocado Kale Smoothie

SERVES 2 Electrolytes and good fats make this smoothie recipe a hit in so many ways. Fuel your body with greens that fight disease and boost your immune system. You'll actually feel the nutrients from this smoothie at work in your body!

1¼ cups coconut water, plus a splash or two

1 avocado, pitted and peeled

3 kale leaves, torn from stem

Juice from ½ lemon

¼ cup ice cubes, optional

1. In a blender, add the coconut water, avocado, kale leaves, lemon juice, and ice cubes, if using. Pulse until smooth, about 30 seconds. If it's too thick, add another splash or two of coconut water until it reaches your desired consistency. Pour into two glasses and add straws for easy drinking!

COOK'S NOTES

INTUITIVE MOMENTS

Kale is the wonder vegetable. You'll find it as a staple at any corner juice stand. But if you really want to go big on nutrients and flavor, this recipe is for you. This smoothie is definitely *smooth*. It's definitely green, too, and gives you all the nutrients of kale, all the beneficial fatty acids of avocado, and the hydrating power of coconut water. It's perfect for breakfast. It's perfect as a replenishment after a workout. It's perfect as a snack for anyone. Drink this smoothie when you're hungry, and I guarantee you will feel alive inside.

HEALTHY IS NOT
TRENDY, NOR IS IT
A LUXURY, SO LET'S
STOP TREATING
IT LIKE IT IS!
SHUT UP AND COOK.

—*Erica Reid*

Acknowledgments

This book has truly been a work of frustration, sweat, and many tears. Oh, and a bit of anxiety. I had NO idea what I was getting myself into when I told my agent for several years over and over again, "My next book is going to be a cookbook." I think I only thought about the pretty photos and what I can cook to put in the book. I did not think nor know about the math and science I needed to get each recipe in the best shape to share with others (they were my two least favorite subjects in school, and ones that I did not pass). It was a challenge, but also such a great test of my ability to stay focused, keep moving forward, and not quit, even when I wanted to. I did not let quitting be the winner.

I am committed to my health and to raising children to thrive and to reach their full optimal health, which is why cooking at home became the only option. It worked better for us and our health than eating out all the time and letting restaurant chefs dictate our menu and our health. I am also committed to helping as many people as possible to reach well-deserved health and to look and feel great, and to learn a little bit extra in the process.

Making this cookbook a reality for any of us was ONLY possible with a strong, winning team. It always takes a village!

GOD, who continues to use me as a vessel—I am grateful for all you have blessed me with and continue to bless me with, and I thank you for this and everything. I love you. Thank you.

Husband—look who's cooking now, baby! I know it's not "Cincin" chili, but hey, I love you because you know it's not and you still devour it anyway. I love watching your expression of shock each time, with each bite. Je t'aime.

Arianna and Addison—thank you for being the best and most honest food tasters and such supporters and the best teachers I have ever had. Thank you for teaching me that, for love and health, I can really make anything if I TRY. Thank you for teaching me not to limit myself. Always choose to feel good and be healthy. Remember, you do have a choice. I love you both deeply.

Aaron, Tony, and Ashley—thank you for loving me and for allowing me to love you.

Mom, Nana, Aunt Carol, Grandma Holton, the beautiful and strong women who are my foundation and backbone and who cooked in my family for me as I was growing up—I guess I was taking note without realizing it. Thank you, thank you, thank you. I love you all so much. Mom, thank you for feeding me well even when you did not feel like coming home and cooking after a full day of work.

Angela and Brigette—I am shocked, too. Especially because I was the cleaner. Sugar and butter on toast and our tea cookies, I guess that was the start. Hahaha—who knew? I did not, that is for sure. Love youz forever.

Daddy—thank you for your friendship and support and making sure Grandma had pickles and sweet potato pie ready for me during each visit. I love you.

Jan Miller—you, my friend, are better than magic. Forever grateful to polka dots and for your constant belief in me and for making "it" possible each time. It only gets better and better. Thank you for being so special and such support for me. You are a gem!

Lacy Lacy Lacy, girl, Lacy Lynch—I have no idea where you came from, but your future is much brighter than you can imagine. Thank you, thank you, thank you for endless loving minutes and hours on this project. There was no such thing as never working and I so appreciate that. You go to bat for what you know is right and I am so grateful you share that with me. Thank you for your strong work ethic and for being exactly YOU. Thank you for caring about health and for being inquisitive and a doer of all things and for making this happen.

The Dupree–Miller team—y'all are rocking over in the south and y'all know what you're doing. Rock on. Thank you for another published book and for your support and dedication on this, too.

Glenn Yeffeth—you believed in me and made my vision come alive. You not only saw a need, but you understood it. I thank you so much for seeing this vison and for knowing there was life for it and allowing me to be creative with it from day one. I am so appreciative. Thank you. BenBella in da house.

Leah Wilson—you are my kind of person: tough and don't let up! That is how we got this done. Thank you for pushing me. More than anything, thank you for not accepting anything just because it was turned in. Thank you for sharing your gifts and knowledge to produce a complete and strong manuscript that makes sense and always keeps the reader in mind, a manuscript that is worthy to share, regardless how many times it took to get it right. Thank you.

Scott Calamar—I loved reading all your notes. Such great humor. Thank you for all the work, insight, comedy, and positive energy you gave this. Thank you for wanting to make this not only meet a deadline, but be great.

Elizabeth Degenhard—thank you for your revisions, talent, and patience in getting this to the next step. Your role is as crucial as any and your time going over this book to get it where it needed to be means much to me. I am very grateful.

Monica Lowry—thank you for being a part of this cookbook that means so much to me.

Kit Sweeney—thank you, thank you, thank you for all you did in making this as close to perfect as perfect can be. Thank you for your time.

Sara Dombrowsky—it took a minute, but boy did we get it! You nailed it. Thank you for the collaboration and creating my vision. I knew what I wanted and you did not miss a beat. I LOVE this cover and I wish I was able to take a selfie when I saw it for the first time. The cover is everything and I love it. Thank you for never giving up on what I was trying to convey and what I saw for this. It is hard to get in someone else's brain to see what they are thinking and wanting, but you got in. Thank you so much.

Adrienne Lang—thank you for staying on me to get this to be what it is and to be where it can actually do what it is capable of doing. You knew how it needed to be, and because of that, we got this. Thank you.

Alicia Kania—thank you for your time and collaboration in this meaningful cookbook.

Rachel Phares—a team requires a team. Thank you for being on this one and making this all it can be.

Heather Butterfield—I am so glad you are still a part of this. Roles may shift but this team did not. Thank you for all you did and continue to do.

Todd Nordstrom—not only was working with you easy and fun, but you shared this journey with me and never gave up, even when you or I felt like we wanted to. Thank you for your patience and being so clear about this vision and understanding it immediately. I thank you for the late and early work calls to get things moving and to meet deadlines and for being available and being a hard worker. You held my hand all the way and never let anything get in the way or stop us from excelling, even when the brakes were applied hard. I am forever grateful for you, and to your family for allowing you the space and time to make this possible. Thank you!!!

Adrianna Adarme—your pretty work and talent drew me in. Thank you for sharing your gift with me. Thank you for your patience, your time, and all you gave to put my recipes in the right form for the reader to follow. It was a long journey, but some things require a bit more baking time. Thank you so much.

Claudia Ficca—you beautiful spirit, you. Thank you for coming into my kitchen and teaching me how to test my own recipes, to get them right to share with the world. I had no idea what I was doing until you came in. I was in tears and wanting to throw in the towel until that beautiful smile and great energy of yours came to the rescue. You were not only patient and fun, you were excited and eager to help me get it right. You shared your passion for what you do with me. You gave me what I needed, when I needed it, and what I needed was YOU. Thank you for showing me how to be organized when testing, and assuring me it was all going to be great, even through my mistakes and the redos. Grazie, bella.

Lisa Bonner—thank you for again for crossing the t's and dotting the i's. Thank you, thank you, and your team, for all your hard work. I appreciate all you did and did not do.

Nicole Garner—wow, wow, wow. Look what you did, my friend. I am so thankful to you for taking every single one of these beautiful, inviting, clear, warm, and delicious photos. Look what YOU did. I am not only proud of what you shared in each photo with me on this project, I am so blessed to have been able to share this journey with you. From CAU to this. You never know what your life path is going to bring you with someone else. Thank you for all the trips you made to shoot

every idea that popped in my gypsy brain. Thank you for not only taking every photo in here and the knock-out cover photo, but for also styling AND shooting the pizza (page 127), rice krispies (page 161), chicken soup (page 121), cast iron skillet (page 1), and cooking utensils (page 7). I love you. THANK YOU for being so great and easy to work with, for having the right attitude, and for getting my vision for each photo and sharing your own. You are a dream to collaborate with. Thank you, thank you, my college ace! I continue to remain grateful and thankful beyond.

Stefan Campbell—my GB, I love you. Thank you for being Mik'e each time you allowed me to cook for you, and for making me cook when you were our house guest. Your constant friendship fuels not only my fashion conversation but my soul. Always a good laugh. I love you, GB.

Hayley Christopher—thank you for spending part of your Thanksgiving break with the photographer, styling these photos to be pretty for their up-close-and-personal photo shoot. You were the food glam team and absolutely perfect for this; I would not have changed or preferred any other food stylist over you for this labor of love. Thank you for your hard, beautiful work and all your time. The styling in each photo is so pretty. Thank you for styling my recipes to perfection. I am very happy with it all. Thank you.

2010 Studios—thank you for opening your studio last minute and during the holidays. I am thankful for you making this shoot possible and providing the space and all we needed to make each photo what it is. Thank you.

Nino Andonis—blessings to you. What a great eye you have, especially for detail. I am so thankful for the work you did editing these photos to perfection and for making it a priority when you did. You are a joy to work with and so pleasant. Thank you for being wonderful, I really appreciate it.

Thank you to the inspiring ladies I admire in many ways who contributed a quote for this book without hesitation. Thank you for your support. I thank you for sharing your voice with us all. I am forever grateful! THANK YOU.

Thank you to every great healthy chef that has ever helped prepare healthy meals in our home and to all the chefs in restaurants that inspired me to go home to try to create my own version of your recipes.

Thank you to all the farmers and grocery stores out there for selling healthy, clean food and knowing how vital that food is for quality health.

Hair and make-up was by no one other than me; I don't like the fuss of all that, so usually I do the bare minimum. Thank you, Erica, for trying to make yourself a bit presentable even when that was work for you!

Thank you for my home team that helps me in my daily life so I can do what I have to do. You are so important. Thank you for leaving your home to come and help in ours.

My sisters, nieces, nephew, and cousins—go for what you want and make it happen. Thank you for being family. I love you all.

Friends—real friends—are rare. I am thankful to my friends who are there for me and support our relationship to make it a real friendship. I love you all for accepting me as I am, for allowing me to be ME, and for supporting anything I get up and say I am going to do or not do. More importantly, thank you for sharing yourselves with me and for all the great laughs yesterday and for more tomorrow. My friends, I laugh and crack up with you and have such a great time with you, and I love cooking for you, so thank YOU!

Last but not least, thank you to YOU for reading this right now—for supporting this cookbook and wanting to achieve better health at home and in your own space. Much love.

This book is in loving memory of Charmayne "Maxee" Maxwell. Thank you for sharing your huge, loving heart with me, especially in my biggest time of need. I love and miss you.

Index

Acorn Squash, Harvest, with Cinnamon Maple Syrup 54

Antioxidant Fruit Salad 24

Apple

    Crisp, Cinnamon Saturday 163

    Pie, Scrumptious Sweet 159

Arame

The Hollywood Bowl 48

Arugula Green Bean Salad, Garden ... 46

Asparagus, Turkey Bacon–Wrapped .. 86

Avocado

    Carrot Salad 67

    Dressing 108

    Guacamole, Gypsy Girl 137

    Kale Smoothie 174

    Pesto Pizza 129

Backyard Pickled Vegetables 51

Balsamic Strawberries with Basil 167

Beet Chips 145

Beverages. *See* Drinks

Black Bean(s)

    Burgers 70

    Dip, Double-Dip 135

    Huevos Rancheros (Egg or Extra-Firm Tofu) with 34

    Mango Salad, with a Kick 62

    Soup 117

    Yum-Yum 55

Black-Eyed Peas, Soul-Warming 61

Bliss Pelau Chicken, Mom's, My Way 91

Blueberry or Chocolate Chip Spelt Muffins 22

Bread. *See also* Muffins

    Challah Vanilla French Toast, Dairy-Free 29

    Focaccia, Modern 143

Nana's Rolls, My Way 132

Breakfast

Antioxidant Fruit Salad 24

Blueberry or Chocolate Chip
Spelt Muffins 22

Carrot Raisin Muffins...................... 25

Cozy Millet and Brown
Rice Porridge.................................. 36

Dairy-Free Challah Vanilla
French Toast 29

Granola Brittle................................ 31

Huevos Rancheros (Egg or
Extra-Firm Tofu) with Black Beans 34

Saturday Morning Spelt and
Oat Pancakes 32

Summer Watermelon Fruit Bowl...... 26

Brittle, Granola 31

Broth 116

Brown Rice

Porridge, Millet and, Cozy 36

Salmon "Sushi" Rolls 104

Brussels Sprouts Chips...................... 145

**Buffalo Chicken Wings,
Game-Day**................................... 82

Bundt Cake, Childhood..................... 157

Bun-less Turkey Burgers.................... 79

Burgers

Black Bean...................................... 70

Lamb, Savory.................................. 98

Turkey, Bun-less............................. 79

Burritos, Tofu Veggie 74

Butternut Soup, Soothing................. 123

Cake, Childhood Bundt..................... 157

Canada Cauliflower 73

Carrot(s)

Avocado Salad 67

Pasta, Zucchini and 58

Pickled.. 51

Raisin Muffins 25

Cauliflower

Canada 73

Pickled 51

Rice Salad, with Green Beans
and Chickpeas.................................. 40

Soup 122

Sushi Rolls, Rice-Free 42

**Challah Vanilla French Toast,
Dairy-Free**... 29

Cheese, Three-Cheese Veggie Pizza .. 128

Cheesecake, Vegan 164

Chicken

Bliss Pelau, Mom's, My Way............ 91

Buffalo Wings, Game-Day 82

City Jerk 76

in the Garden, LA's Favorite 85

Soup, Shredded "Soup-Kitchen"... 120

**Chickpeas, Cauliflower Rice
Salad with Green Beans and**.......... 40

Childhood Bundt Cake...................... 157

Chips 144

Beet 145

Brussels Sprouts............................. 145

Kale...119

Mushroom 144

Zucchini 144

Chocolate

Glaze... 152

Truffles, Decadent.......................... 166

Chocolate Chip

Cookies, with Crispy Kale 149

Spelt Muffins 22

Cider Maple Vinaigrette 113

Cinnamon

Apple Crisp, Saturday 163

Maple Syrup, Harvest
Acorn Squash with 54

City Jerk Chicken............................... 76

Coconut Rice 64

Cod en Papillote, Miso 103

Collard Green(s)

    Green Juice 170

    Wraps, Mother Earth 57

**Cookies, Chocolate Chip,
with Crispy Kale** 149

Cooling Watermelon Juice 172

**Cozy Millet and Brown
Rice Porridge** 36

Cream, Tofu 117

**Crispy Kale, Chocolate Chip
Cookies with** 149

Crudités, Snack-Time, Tofu Dip with 38

**Dairy-Free Challah Vanilla
French Toast** 29

Decadent Chocolate Truffles 166

Desserts

    Balsamic Strawberries with Basil 167

    Childhood Bundt Cake 157

    Chocolate Chip Cookies with
Crispy Kale 149

    Cinnamon Saturday Apple Crisp ... 163

    Decadent Chocolate Truffles 166

    Grandma's Nondairy Sweet
Potato Pie 150

    Guilt-Free Doughnuts 152

    Nondairy Strawberry Ice Cream 154

    Pineapple Lemon Granita 156

    Raspberry Strawberry Soup 168

    Scrumptious Sweet Apple Pie 159

    Soy Butter Rice Krispies® Cups 160

    Vegan Cheesecake 164

    Watermelon Granita 153

Dip

    Black Bean, Double-Dip 135

    Tofu, with Crudités, Snack-Time 38

Double-Dip Black Bean Dip 135

Doughnuts, Guilt-Free 152

Dressing

    Avocado 108

    Lemon 110

    Maple Cider Vinaigrette 113

    Salad, Herbed 111

Drinks

    Avocado Kale Smoothie 174

    Cooling Watermelon Juice 172

    Green Juice 170

    Raspberry Sorbet with
Sparkling Water 171

    Tropical Fruit Smoothie 173

**Egg, Huevos Rancheros, with
Black Beans** 34

Family Turkey Meatloaf 88

Fennel and Orange Salad 45

Fish

    Ginger Salmon 100

    Gluten-Free Salmon Pea Pasta 105

    Miso Cod en Papillote 103

    Salmon "Sushi" Rolls 104

Focaccia Bread, Modern 143

**French-Style Radishes with
Nondairy Butter** 146

**French Toast, Dairy-Free
Challah Vanilla** 29

Fries

    Parsnip 140

    Sweet Potato, with Rosemary 139

Fruit

    Bowl, Summer Watermelon 26

    Salad, Antioxidant 24

    Smoothie, Tropical 173

Fry-Free Veggie Spring Rolls 68

Game-Day Buffalo Chicken Wings 82

Garden Arugula Green Bean Salad 46

Garlic Boost Spread 136

Gazpacho, Home-Run 39

Ginger Salmon 100

Glaze
Chocolate 152
Lemon.................................... 157
Gluten-Free Salmon Pea Pasta 105
**Grandma's Nondairy Sweet
Potato Pie** 150
Granita
Pineapple Lemon 156
Watermelon.............................. 153
Granola Brittle 31
Green Bean(s)
Cauliflower Rice Salad with
Chickpeas and.............................. 40
Salad, Garden Arugula..................... 46
Green Juice 170
Green Soup 119
Guacamole, Gypsy Girl 137
Guilt-Free Doughnuts........................ 152
Gypsy Girl Guacamole 137

**Harvest Acorn Squash with
Cinnamon Maple Syrup** 54
Herbed Salad Dressing 111
The Hollywood Bowl 48
Home-Run Gazpacho........................... 39
Honeymoon Salsa 141
**Huevos Rancheros (Egg or
Extra-Firm Tofu) with Black Beans**... 34

Ice Cream, Nondairy Strawberry 154

Jerk Chicken, City............................... 76
Juice
Green.................................... 170
Watermelon, Cooling..................... 172

Kale
Avocado Smoothie.......................174
Chips 119
Crispy, Chocolate Chip
Cookies with.............................. 149

Green Juice 170
Pesto.. 129
Soup..119
Kelp Noodle Stir-Fry...................... 65
**Kielbasa with Sauerkraut,
Mom's Staple**................................. 95

Lamb
Burgers, Savory 98
Chops, Rosemary 96
Lemon
Dressing 110
Glaze...................................... 157
Pineapple Granita 156
Load 'em Up Vegetable Stir-Fry......... 52

Mama's Turkey Meatballs 81
**Mango Black Bean Salad
with a Kick** 62
Maple Cider Vinaigrette 113
**Maple Cinnamon Syrup, Harvest
Acorn Squash with**...................... 54
Meatballs, Mama's Turkey 81
Meatloaf, Family Turkey....................88
Meats. *See also* Poultry
Mom's Staple Kielbasa with
Sauerkraut 95
Rosemary Lamb Chops.................... 96
Savory Lamb Burgers...................... 98
**Millet and Brown Rice Porridge,
Cozy** 36
Miso Cod en Papillote...................... 103
Modern Focaccia Bread 143
**Mom's Bliss Pelau Chicken,
My Way** 91
**Mom's Staple Kielbasa with
Sauerkraut** 95
Mother Earth Collard Green Wraps.....57
Muffins
Blueberry or Chocolate Chip Spelt ...22

Carrot Raisin.................................... 25
Mushroom Chips............................... 144

Nana's Rolls, My Way 132
New York Bowl.................................... 47
**Nondairy Butter, French-Style
Radishes with** 146
Nondairy Strawberry Ice Cream 154
**Nondairy Sweet Potato Pie,
Grandma's** 150
Noodle(s)
Kelp, Stir-Fry.................................... 65
Load 'em Up Vegetable Stir-Fry....... 52
Mother Earth Collard Green Wraps ... 57
Nori
Rice-Free Cauliflower Sushi Rolls..... 42
Toasted, and Sea Salt Popcorn 134

**Oat and Spelt Pancakes,
Saturday Morning** 32
Onion, Red, Pickled............................ 46
Orange and Fennel Salad 45

**Pancakes, Spelt and Oat,
Saturday Morning** 32
Parsley
Green Juice 170
Parsnip Fries.................................... 140
Pasta. *See also* Noodle(s)
Salmon Pea, Gluten-Free 105
Zucchini and Carrot......................... 58
Pea Salmon Pasta, Gluten-Free........ 105
Pesto
Avocado Pizza 129
Kale... 129
Pickled Carrots 51
Pickled Cauliflower............................ 51
Pickled Radishes 51
Pickled Red Onion 46
Pickled Vegetables, Backyard 51

Pie
Apple, Scrumptious Sweet 159
Sweet Potato, Grandma's
Nondairy....................................... 150
Pineapple Lemon Granita 156
Pizza
Arianna and Addison's, With Love ... 126
Pesto Avocado 129
Three-Cheese Veggie 128
Plum Sauce 114
**Popcorn, Toasted Nori and
Sea Salt** 134
**Porridge, Millet and Brown
Rice, Cozy** 36
Poultry
Chicken, City Jerk 76
Chicken, Mom's Bliss Pelau,
My Way... 91
Chicken in the Garden,
LA's Favorite 85
Chicken Wings, Buffalo,
Game-Day.....................................82
Turkey Bacon–Wrapped
Asparagus 86
Turkey Burgers, Bun-less................. 79
Turkey Meatballs, Mama's............... 81
Turkey Meatloaf, Family 88
Turkey Tacos.................................. 77

Quinoa
New York Bowl 47

Radishes
French-Style, with Nondairy
Butter 146
Pickled 51
Raisin Carrot Muffins......................... 25
Raspberry
Sorbet, with Sparkling Water.........171
Strawberry Soup 168

Red Onion, Pickled 46

Rice

Brown, Porridge, Cozy Millet and.... 36

Coconut.. 64

Salmon "Sushi" Rolls 104

Rice-Free Cauliflower Sushi Rolls 42

Rice Krispies® Cups, Soy Butter 160

Rice vermicelli

Load 'em Up Vegetable Stir-Fry....... 52

Mother Earth Collard Green Wraps ... 57

Rolls, Nana's, My Way 132

Rosemary

Lamb Chops 96

Sweet Potato Fries with 139

Salad

Arugula Green Bean, Garden 46

Avocado Carrot................................ 67

Black Bean Mango, with a Kick........ 62

Cauliflower Rice, with Green
Beans and Chickpeas 40

Fruit, Antioxidant 24

Orange and Fennel 45

Salad Dressing

Herbed 111

Maple Cider Vinaigrette 113

Salmon

Ginger 100

Pea Pasta, Gluten-Free 105

"Sushi" Rolls 104

Salsa, Honeymoon 141

Saturday Morning Spelt and
Oat Pancakes................................... 32

Sauce

Plum...114

Teriyaki 112

Sauerkraut, Kielbasa with,
Mom's Staple................................... 95

Savory Lamb Burgers 98

Scrumptious Sweet Apple Pie 159

Sea vegetables

The Hollywood Bowl 48

Kelp Noodle Stir-Fry 65

Rice-Free Cauliflower Sushi Rolls 42

Salmon "Sushi" Rolls 104

Toasted Nori and Sea
Salt Popcorn 134

Shredded "Soup-Kitchen"
Chicken Soup 120

Smoothie

Avocado Kale 174

Tropical Fruit 173

Snacks

Chips 144

Double-Dip Black Bean Dip 135

French-Style Radishes with
Nondairy Butter 146

Garlic Boost Spread 136

Gypsy Girl Guacamole 137

Honeymoon Salsa 141

Modern Focaccia Bread................. 143

Nana's Rolls, My Way 132

Parsnip Fries 140

Sweet Potato Fries with
Rosemary....................................... 139

Toasted Nori and Sea
Salt Popcorn 134

Snack-Time Tofu Dip with Crudités.... 38

Soothing Butternut Soup.................. 123

Sorbet, Raspberry, with
Sparkling Water 171

Soul-Warming Black-Eyed Peas 61

Soup

Black Bean....................................117

Broth..116

Butternut, Soothing 123

Cauliflower 122

Chicken, Shredded
"Soup-Kitchen" 120

Gazpacho, Home-Run 39

Green.................................119

Kale.................................119

Raspberry Strawberry 168

Soy Butter Rice Krispies® Cups 160

Spelt

Muffins, Blueberry or
Chocolate Chip 22

Pancakes, Oat and, Saturday
Morning................................32

Spread, Garlic Boost 136

Spring Rolls, Veggie, Fry-Free.............68

Stir-Fry

Kelp Noodle 65

Vegetable, Load 'em Up 52

Strawberry(-ies)

Balsamic, with Basil 167

Ice Cream, Nondairy 154

Raspberry Soup...........................168

Topping 164

Summer Watermelon Fruit Bowl 26

Sushi ("Shushi") Rolls

Rice-Free Cauliflower.....................42

Salmon..............................104

Sweet Apple Pie, Scrumptious 159

Sweet Potato

Fries, with Rosemary 139

Pie, Grandma's Nondairy 150

**Syrup, Cinnamon Maple, Harvest
Acorn Squash with**..........................54

Tacos, Turkey.................................77

Teriyaki Sauce 112

Three-Cheese Veggie Pizza 128

**Toasted Nori and Sea
Salt Popcorn**..............................134

Tofu

Cream................................117

Dip, with Crudités, Snack-Time........38

Extra-Firm, Huevos Rancheros,
with Black Beans 34

Fry-Free Veggie Spring Rolls 68

Veggie Burritos 74

Topping, Strawberry 164

Tropical Fruit Smoothie.....................173

Truffles, Decadent Chocolate...........166

Turkey

Burgers, Bun-less 79

Meatballs, Mama's 81

Meatloaf, Family......................88

Tacos.................................77

Turkey Bacon–Wrapped Asparagus....86

Vegan Cheesecake 164

Vegetable(s). *See also* Veggie

Backyard Pickled 51

Crudités, Snack-Time, Tofu
Dip with 38

Stir-Fry, Load 'em Up 52

Vegetarian

Avocado Carrot Salad......................67

Backyard Pickled Vegetables..........51

Black Bean Burgers 70

Black Bean Mango Salad, with
a Kick 62

Canada Cauliflower..........................73

Cauliflower Rice Salad, with
Green Beans and Chickpeas...........40

Coconut Rice.............................64

Fry-Free Veggie Spring Rolls 68

Garden Arugula Green
Bean Salad............................46

Harvest Acorn Squash with
Cinnamon Maple Syrup 54

The Hollywood Bowl......................48

Home-Run Gazpacho 39

Kelp Noodle Stir-Fry 65

Load 'em Up Vegetable Stir-Fry.......52

Mother Earth Collard
Green Wraps 57

New York Bowl 47

Orange and Fennel Salad 45

Rice-Free Cauliflower Sushi Rolls..... 42

Snack-Time Tofu Dip with
Crudités... 38

Soul-Warming Black-Eyed Peas 61

Tofu Veggie Burritos 74

Yum-Yum Black Beans 55

Zucchini and Carrot Pasta............... 58

Veggie. *See also* Vegetable(s)

Burritos, Tofu.................................... 74

Pizza, Three-Cheese 128

Spring Rolls, Fry-Free....................... 68

Vinaigrette, Maple Cider 113

Watermelon

Fruit Bowl, Summer........................... 26

Granita... 153

Juice, Cooling.................................. 172

**With Love, Arianna and
Addison's Pizza** 126

Wraps, Mother Earth Collard Green ...57

Yum-Yum Black Beans 55

Zucchini

Chips 144

Pasta, Carrot and 58

About the Author

Did You Know?

I am so thankful that you are reading this book and trying these recipes with me!

Erica Reid is founder of a health-conscious lifestyle brand and conscious living movement geared at simple everyday ways to improve and nurture your life for yourself and your loved ones.

Erica is mother to Arianna and Addison, and her commitment to health and dedication to mothering led her to write her first book, *The Thriving Child*—a much-needed nourishment guide for parents and those with day-to-day involvement with children. Her versatility and global brand speaks to women of all backgrounds who are inspired toward a sustainable and vibrant life.

Erica's roots go back to Colorado, where she was one of three daughters raised by a single mom. She worked three jobs to put herself through college and fed her gypsy spirit by learning how to survive on her own in Atlanta, Paris, California, and Greece before finally settling in New York and then Los Angeles, where she currently lives with her husband, music mogul and visionary Antonio "LA" Reid, and their two children.